You Are Not Alone
The Challenge and Triumphs of Dyslexia

Petronila A. Ngeka

You Are Not Alone
Authored by Petronila A. Ngeka
Copyright © Petronila A. Ngeka 2025
ISBN: 978-1-0681515-2-1

Edited by Marcia M Publishing House Editorial Team. Cover design, printing & binding: Marcia M Publishing House Ltd. Published by Marcia M. Spence of Marcia M Publishing House Ltd. On behalf of Petronila A. Ngeka, In West Bromwich, West Midlands the United KINGDOM B71.
All rights reserved, Petronila A. Ngeka 2025
All images are the property of Petronila A. Ngeka, who holds the right to publish this work. Petronila A. Ngeka asserts the moral right to be identified as the author of this work. The opinions expressed in this published work are those of the author and do not reflect the opinions of Marcia M Publishing House or its editorial team.

This book is sold subject to the conditions it is not, by way of trade or otherwise, lent, hired out or otherwise circulated in any form of binding or cover other than that in which it is published. No part of this publication may be reproduced, stored in a retrieval system or transmitted in any form or by any means (electronic, mechanical, photocopying, recording or otherwise) without prior written permission from the Author.

A copy of this publication is legally deposited at The British Library.

www.marciampublishinghouse.com

Content page

Introduction 5

Chapter One: What is Dyslexia? 8

Chapter Two: My Dyslexia Story 46

Chapter Three: The Survival of a Dyslexic Nurse 54

Chapter Four: Guide to Managing Dyslexia 83

Chapter Five: Guide for Parents 89

Chapter Six: What can be done
to embrace dyslexia? 93

Chapter Seven: Prejudice of Dyslexia 102

Chapter Eight: Dyslexia is a Gift 111

Chapter Nine: The role parents,
teachers play in Dyslexia. 125

Chapter Ten: You are not Alone. 134

Acknowledgements

First and foremost, I want to honour my father, **Mr. John Asang**, whose tireless support throughout my school years and unwavering belief in my potential made it possible for me to transition to the UK. Your sacrifices laid the foundation for everything I have become.

To my loving mother, **Justina Asang**, thank you for being my source of comfort during my lowest moments. You have always been there to lift me up when I felt like giving up on my dreams.

To my son, **Hanson Tabe**, thank you for unknowingly guiding me to the discovery of my dyslexia. It was through you that I began to understand why I struggled in school and, in doing so; I found healing and purpose in writing this book to share the fact that dyslexia is genetic in African heritage as other backgrounds.

To my daughter, **Nila Tabe** your energy, enthusiasm, and unique spirit light up our lives. You are a beautiful reminder that we each walk a different path, and yours is refreshingly bold and joyful.

A heartfelt thank you to **Adele Njikam** for overseeing the completion of this book. Your guidance and encouragement were invaluable.

To my beloved sister, **Abigail Tala**, you are deeply missed. You were not only my sister but also a fellow dyslexic and a cherished friend. Your impact on my life is immeasurable, and your memory lives on through these pages.

Dr. Blaise Nkwenti, thank you for being a wise and dependable mentor. Your support continues to shape my journey.

To my wonderful family, especially **Mrs Ambe Catherine, Evete Ngewie, Catherine Azah, Asang Quinta Ngum, Asang Beverley,** enduring love of family.

To the incredible **team behind me,** thank you for contributing to my success story. I couldn't have done it without your dedication and belief in the vision.

Gratitude also goes to my **close community**, whose constant encouragement reminds me that I am never alone.

To my amazing **staff**, especially my **admin team**, thank you for your commitment, resilience, and faith in the mission we share.

And finally, thank you to **Marcia M. Spence of Marcia M. Publishing**, my wonderful publisher, for bringing this dream to life. Your belief in my story made "You Are Not Alone" a reality.

With deepest appreciation,

Introduction

The British Dyslexia Association reports that approximately 10% of the UK population has dyslexia, with 4% exhibiting the most serious form. However, this has been argued to be underestimated, with the accurate figure more likely to be around 16% of the population, or over 11.5 million people. I was inspired to write this book I the pandemic 2021, to share something close to my heart the world and journey with dyslexia, which is finally out now in 2025. As I write this back I reflected on data by British Dyslexia Association estimates that one in five adults possesses the reading comprehension of an eleven-year-old. Of these estimates, over 80% will go undiagnosed and untreated.

1. A lifelong problem, dyslexia, depending on its spectrum, can present daily challenges. Such as misplacing items like car keys, unable to tidy up the house or office organisation, doing laundry, cooking and planning, which can affect the normal functioning of those affected.

2. There's a lot of misconceptions and ignorance associated with dyslexia, which leads to it going undiagnosed into adulthood.

3. I wrote this book because of my personal journey as a dyslexic mother, and in raising a dyslexic child. I did not find out I had dyslexia until much later in my life, at age 30. It took a research study for me to understand who I am, and this has put me in a better place. This book aims to help parents, teachers, and dyslexics understand dyslexia and enhance the lives of those with it.

4. This book helps you learn, find answers, and overcome prejudice. It is a guide to help you understand the tough but exciting maze called dyslexia.

Chapter One
What is Dyslexia?

> Dyslexia has struggles but is beautiful, creative, and a gift. Find the talent within your disability.
>
> Petronila Ngeka

Dyslexia is a learning difficulty that affects the skills involved in accurate and fluent word reading and spelling. People with dyslexia often struggle with sounds in words, recalling things, and processing language quickly.

Dyslexia is a neurological condition thought to affect a part of the brain called the cerebellum (which is the brain within the brain). The cerebellum is responsible for speech, spelling, speed and reading skills. Simply put, someone with dyslexia has difficulty processing letters and sounds, which makes it difficult to read.

Reading is an acquired skill, which begins in some cases before a child is born – some children are read to by their parents while they are in the womb. In the real sense, reading may begin in the early years of a child or when the child begins kindergarten. For children, reading begins slowly, with the alphabet introduced to them. Learning how to read then progresses to small words and then short sentences. This learning soon develops, and children can read without supervision. However, for children with dyslexia, reading doesn't come easily; learning to read becomes a slow and horrendous experience. This continues into adulthood. The severity of this disorder ranges from mild to serious.

Although dyslexia cannot be cured, it is treatable, but the sooner it is treated – in childhood – the better the outcome. However, it is never too late for dyslexia to be treated.

The Dyslexia Centre of Utah in the United States suggests that 70-80% of people with poor reading skills are probably dyslexic. One in five students, 15-20% of the population, has a language-based learning disability. The British Dyslexia Association (BDA) stated that 10-15% of the UK population has dyslexia, which impacts 1.3 million young people in education and up to 9.9 million people in the UK.

Several learning disabilities exist, including Attention Deficit Hyperactivity Disorder, dysphagia, and processing deficits; however, dyslexia is the most prevalent language-based learning disability.

Signs of Dyslexia

Children and adults with dyslexia have the following problems with academic work:
1. Reading and spelling below grade level.
2. Many spelling errors.
3. Spending a long-time completing classwork and homework.
4. Difficulty remembering or understanding what one has heard.
5. Rereading sentences several times to understand words and the meaning of texts.
6. Difficulty finding the right words when writing or speaking.
7. Finding it difficult to learn a foreign language.

Causes of Dyslexia

There's no definitive answer to dyslexia's cause; however, researchers have pinpointed contributing factors. The causes could also vary with the type of dyslexia.

1. Genetics is one of the major causes of dyslexia. Basically, it runs in the family. About 49% of parents with dyslexia will see their children inherit the disability, and about 40% of siblings will experience reading challenges. Thus, with dyslexia, there is a strong likelihood your child will also be affected, and a family member shares the condition.
2. The brain is a precious part of the human body. It serves as the thinking box. A malfunction in the brain affects the normal functioning of anyone. Research indicates that individuals

with dyslexia engage different brain regions during reading, unlike those without dyslexia.

Types of Dyslexia

Although no institution has created a list of the types of dyslexia, many have agreed on the different ways people struggle with reading.

Understanding How Adults and Children Experience Dyslexia Differently.

Dyslexia is a lifelong condition, but how it manifests and impacts daily life can vary between children and adults. Grasping these differences is vital for offering effective assistance and promoting inclusivity. In this exploration, we will delve into the different types of dyslexia, their effects, and how these experiences differ across age groups.

1. Phonological Dyslexia

Also known as dysphonetic or auditory dyslexia, this is believed to be the most common form of dyslexia. This involves having difficulty recognising individual letter sounds in a word and then blending those sounds into a word. It's difficult to break words into syllables and to connect letters and words to the sounds they correspond to. Consider all the things you read daily: messages, emails, documents, and other materials. I knew I had dyslexia when I started using social media trying to contribute and my-self heard and seen. The challenge of misspelling hit me in the face. I remember seeing somewhere that we read many thousands of words per day. Now consider that you are a person with dyslexia trying to read just one of those thousands of words. The word you are considering is "unfortunately." You can translate the sound at the beginning as "un" and the sound at the end as "ly,". You cannot understand the middle sounds and must take a visual guess at the phrase. The result is something like "unforchently."

Phonological dyslexia, also known as dysphonetic or auditory dyslexia, is the most common form. It involves difficulty in recognising individual sounds within words and blending them to form words. This makes it hard to break words into syllables or match letters to sounds.

Example in Daily Life: A person with phonological dyslexia might encounter the word "unfortunately." They can decipher the beginning ("un") and the end ("ly") but struggle with the middle sounds. This can lead to mispronunciations such as "unforchently." when I send messages to some of the WhatsApp groups. I make these errors and people will just ignore me. I would consider myself disregarded and prevent engagement. But self-awareness is good. Those who are not dyslexic may not understand.

In Children: Phonological dyslexia is often identified when children struggle with early reading skills. When I was a child and I had to read out loud in class. My leg will become jellylike and my voice will shake. I detested reading; however, audiobooks are available today to help children enhance their learning abilities.

In Adults: I never read a book for leisure my entire life until I embarked on entrepreneurship. I read the book, Millionaire Success Habit, by Dean Graziosi. As an adult with phonological dyslexia may struggle with a high volume of writing, this was audio. Reviewing dense material, for example work reports or legal documents, can be draining. I signed a business contract without carefully reading it because the content was dense with lots of small print. I sought advice from a third party and discovered clauses in the contract that were not fulfilled. However, they often develop coping strategies, such as relying on context or memorising word shapes. For example, I confuse the word mine with mind. I am unable to read capitals; I must memorise them.

2. Surface Dyslexia

People with this condition (also called dyseidetic or visual dyslexia) have trouble recognising words. They take a long time to recognise a certain word, even if the word is being seen daily. It is important to keep in mind that dyslexia rarely involves a problem with vision or eyesight. A person's brain processes letters, numbers, and words in its own way.

This condition also includes the inability to read words that are spelt differently from how they are pronounced. Words that can prove challenging to people with surface dyslexia might include "yacht," "thorough," and "subtle." Surface dyslexia, also called dyseidetic or visual dyslexia, is characterised by difficulty recognising words by sight. Individuals with this type struggle to read irregularly spelled words and rely heavily on phonetic decoding, which can be unreliable for words like "yacht" or "thorough."

In Children: Children with surface dyslexia may be slow readers because they cannot instantly recognise common words. They often rely on sounding out words, which can be problematic for irregular spellings. This can lead to frustration in both academic and social settings, especially when peers read more fluently.

In Adults: Adults with surface dyslexia may continue to read slowly and struggle with words they haven't encountered frequently. This can affect professional performance at work, especially in roles requiring fast reading or comprehension of complex texts. I remember one day when I called my colleague whose name was Dr. Cox and I said Dr. Cock; it was embracing but I could not under him smiling at me and him repeating to me how to sound his name then I immediately told him I was dyslexic and apologised.

3. Rapid Automatic Naming Dyslexia

For those living with this type of dyslexia, recognition of letters and numbers is slow. It may take longer for the person's brain to process the information, which may lead to a slower reading speed. **Rapid Automatic Naming Dyslexia** affects the speed at which a person recognises letters, numbers, or words. It is not about understanding the material, but about how quickly the brain processes visual information. For people with this type of dyslexia, recognising and naming letters or words takes longer. Which can cause slower reading speeds and a range of challenges in academic, social, and professional settings.

In Children

Children with rapid automatic naming dyslexia are often labelled as "slow readers," even when they understand the material. The issue lies in their ability to decode and recognise the words they see.

This can make schoolwork more stressful and it affects their confidence in the classroom.

Example:

Imagine a child named Samuel, a bright and curious 10-year-old who loves learning about outer space. When his class reads aloud from a science textbook, Samuel struggles to keep up. His peers finish reading their sections, but Samuel stumbles through, pausing often as he slowly decodes each word. By the time it's his turn to read, he's already nervous and frustrated, knowing his classmates are waiting for him to finish. This isn't because he doesn't understand the material; in fact, Samuel could tell you all about black holes and the solar system. It's because his brain needs extra time to process the letters and words on the page.

When timed reading exercises are introduced, the pressure becomes even more overwhelming. Teachers might misinterpret his slower pace as a lack of effort or capability. Over time, the constant pressure and comparisons can make Samuel reluctant to take part, even in subjects he enjoys. His self-esteem takes a hit, and he may view reading as something he's "bad at," even though it's just the speed of recognition that's the issue.

In Adults
Adults with rapid automatic naming dyslexia may struggle in fast-paced situations that demand quick reading. Tasks like skimming emails, reading instructions, or even identifying street signs can take longer than they would for others. This can

create frustration, especially in professional settings where efficiency is highly valued.

Example:

Consider Angela, a graphic designer who is highly creative and skilled at her job. Angela is very good at developing new ideas and creating visual content, but she finds it hard to read fast. When she receives a detailed email from a client with last-minute changes, she needs more time to process the instructions. Angela rereads the message multiple times to ensure she hasn't missed any details. This delay causes her anxiety, particularly when facing stringent deadlines.

In her personal life, Angela faces similar challenges. When driving in an unfamiliar city, she has difficulty recognising street names and navigating complex signs. This often makes her hesitant to drive alone in new areas. Over time, Angela has developed strategies like using voice-to-text software and relying on navigation apps to help her cope. While these tools are helpful, she sometimes experiences the need to hide her struggles to avoid being judged as inefficient or slow.

Impact on Confidence and Coping Strategies

Children and adults with rapid automatic naming (RAN) dyslexia are often wrongly seen as slow learners, despite their normal intelligence. The constant need to put in extra effort to keep up with peers can lead to frustration and a sense of inadequacy.

For Children: Samuel's teacher might notice his struggles and introduce accommodations. like allowing more time for reading or using audiobooks to supplement text-based learning. With encouragement and support, Samuel could regain confidence and rediscover his love for science.

For Adults: Angela finds success by advocating for herself in the workplace. To help her colleagues appreciate her talents, she explained her need for more time and showcased her creativity. Angela's use of technology also allows her to thrive in both her professional and personal life.

Thus, rapid automatic naming dyslexia is not a measure of intelligence or capability. Instead, it reflects how the brain processes visual information. With awareness, support, and the right tools, individuals with this type of dyslexia can succeed and shine in their own time and in their own way.

4. Double Deficit Dyslexia

The presence of more than one type of dyslexia is not infrequent. Phonological dyslexia and problems with rapid naming frequently appear together. Double deficit dyslexia results from the presence of both deficits.

A person may be diagnosed with dyslexia, but also exhibit Dyscalculia, which is difficulty with math. Dysgraphia, which is a difficulty writing.

Left-right disorder, which is trouble telling left from right. Double Deficit Dyslexia is one of the most challenging forms of dyslexia, as it combines the difficulties of phonological dyslexia (problems with recognising sounds in words). Rapid naming deficit dyslexia (slowness in identifying letters, numbers, or words). Together, these deficits make reading, writing, and processing written information arduous, impacting academic, professional, and personal lives.

In Children

Children with double deficit dyslexia often face overwhelming challenges in literacy. The difficulties in decoding sounds, recognising letters, and processing words make keeping pace with their peers almost impossible. These struggles can lead to feelings of failure, social isolation, and frustration. However, with the right support and intervention, these children can still excel in other areas and thrive.

Example:

Meet Emma, a bright and imaginative eight-year-old who loves drawing and storytelling. While her classmates are breezing through their reading lessons, Emma is stuck trying to sound out the simplest of words. When asked to read aloud, she stumbles over sentences, mispronounces words, and loses her place. It's not that Emma doesn't understand the story; she can explain the plot better than most. But the effort required to decode each word exhausts her and leaves her falling behind.

Emma considers herself slow and inadequate because her classmates finish reading before her. During group work, she avoids taking part in activities that require reading or writing, which isolates her. Emma's teachers may mistake her anxiety and lack of participation for laziness, not realising her struggles.

Despite the challenges, Emma's creativity shines through her artwork and oral storytelling. A supportive teacher introduces Emma to audiobooks and encourages her to illustrate scenes from the stories she listens to. This approach allows Emma to engage with literacy in a way that suits her strengths, building her confidence.

In Adults

Adults with double deficit dyslexia often carry the struggles they faced as children into their adult lives. Many develop avoidance behaviours, steering clear of reading-intensive tasks or roles. People find clever ways around problems, like using technology or asking for help. Although helpful, these strategies don't solve the root problems, so feelings of inadequacy or frustration may persist.

Example:

John, a 35-year-old chef, is a master of his craft in the kitchen. His recipes are renowned for their creativity, and his ability to lead a team is unparalleled. Reading is something John tries to avoid, for example, reviewing invoices or following recipes. While John develops menu ideas and tastes, his sous-chef handles the menu descriptions.

John uses voice-to-text apps to write emails and audiobooks to learn about culinary trends. Despite his success, he sometimes experiences shame when he must ask a colleague to help him read a printed schedule or correct a written order. He fears being judged or seen as less capable, even though his dyslexia doesn't affect his culinary talents.

One day, John opens up to his team about his struggles. To his surprise, they are supportive and even suggest tools and strategies to make his work easier. This acceptance boosts John's confidence and eases his burden of concealing his dyslexia.

Impact on Confidence and Coping Strategies

Double deficit dyslexia can undermine self-esteem in both children and adults. The constant struggle to keep up with literacy demands often leads to frustration, anxiety, and a sense of inadequacy. People with this condition may question their abilities without proper understanding and support.

For Children:

Emma's journey underscores the importance of early intervention and understanding. Emma learns to embrace her unique learning style with the help of audiobooks, personalised teaching strategies, and a focus on her creative strengths. This support not only improves her literacy skills but also rebuilds her confidence.

For Adults: John's experience highlights the power of self-advocacy and technology. By using speech-to-text tools and relying on his team for support, he transforms his challenges into manageable obstacles. His openness about his dyslexia also fosters a more inclusive and understanding workplace culture.

Finding Strength in Other Abilities.

People with double deficit dyslexia may struggle with reading and writing but often shine in other skills. Many are creative, innovative, and skilled in fields like art, music, design, and hands-on trades.

Example: Emma grows up to become a graphic designer, using her artistic talents to tell stories through visuals rather than words. She champions dyslexic children, sharing her experiences and promoting diverse learning.

John uses his cooking and speaking skills to inspire others in his new cooking classes. His openness about his dyslexia becomes a source of strength, encouraging others to overcome their own challenges.

Finally, double deficit dyslexia is one of the most challenging forms of dyslexia, but it doesn't define an individual's potential. Emma and similar children can flourish with early intervention and support.

For adults like John, self-advocacy and support systems can turn obstacles into opportunities. Ultimately, the key is recognising that dyslexia is not a limitation but a different way of learning, thinking, and succeeding.

Effects of Dyslexia Across Age Groups

Dyslexia affects various aspects of life, and these effects can manifest differently in children and adults because of differences in responsibilities, coping mechanisms, and societal expectations.

1. Academic and Professional Performance

- **In Children:** Dyslexia often affects a child's grades, as reading and writing form the foundation of most subjects. Difficulty keeping pace with others can cause repeated setbacks, fostering a negative self-perception. Children

may require additional tutoring or individualised education plans (IEPs) to succeed academically.
- **In Adults**: Adults with life experiences, in the workplace, adults with dyslexia may face challenges in roles requiring extensive reading or writing. They might skip promotions in fields like health and social care due to the extensive documentation required for evidence-based practice. As a nurse, I never envisioned progressing from a band 5 role to a band 7 or 8, even in positions that require advanced literacy skills, thus hindering career advancement for myself and others facing similar obstacles. However, many people like me thrive in creative or technical fields where their strengths, such as problem-solving and innovation, are valued, and this meant I was able to create three business brands and write books on this journey

to support other. This brings me to what Horace Mann said, "You should be ashamed to die if you have not contributed to mankind.

2. Self-Esteem and Mental Health

- **In Children:** Being teased or misunderstood in school can lead to low self-esteem. Dyslexic children may internalise the belief that they are "not smart," even when they excel in other areas, like sports or art. This can cause withdrawal or reluctance to take part in classroom activities.
- **In Adults:** Adults may carry the scars of childhood experiences, leading to ongoing self-doubt. Undiagnosed dyslexia can be damaging, as adults may be frustrated by their unexplained difficulties. Depression and anxiety are

common, especially in high-pressure environments.

3. Social Interactions

- **In Children:** Dyslexic children may avoid group activities that involve reading aloud or writing. They may also become distracted in class, drawing negative attention from teachers and peers. This can hinder the development of social skills and friendships.
- **In Adults:** Adults may shy away from social situations that highlight their difficulties, such as book clubs or public speaking events. Despite dyslexia, many adults build strong relationships using their empathy and creativity.

4. Compensatory Strengths

- **In Children:** Dyslexic children often excel in non-academic areas, such as sports, music, or art. These activities provide an outlet for self-expression and a chance to shine, boosting their confidence.
- **In Adults:** Adults with dyslexia frequently leverage their strengths in problem-solving, big-picture thinking, and creativity. Dyslexia doesn't stop many adults from thriving as entrepreneurs, inventors, or artists.

Lessons from Dyslexia: Opportunities for Growth and Support

Dyslexia, though challenging, offers opportunities for personal growth and societal advancement. Knowing its impact on all ages helps us build a more inclusive space for children and adults.

1. Early Intervention and Support

Identifying dyslexia early in childhood allows for targeted interventions that can improve outcomes. Dyslexic children benefit from programmes using phonics, multisensory learning, and personalised teaching.

2. Workplace Accommodations

Accommodations like flexible deadlines and assistive technology can help dyslexic employees succeed. Recognising the unique strengths of dyslexic employees can also enhance workplace diversity and innovation.

3. Promoting Dyslexia Awareness

Raising awareness about dyslexia helps combat stigma and fosters understanding. A better understanding of this condition can be achieved through training in schools and workplaces.

4. Building Confidence

Both children and adults with dyslexia benefit from environments that celebrate their strengths. Encouraging achievement in non-academic areas and providing emotional support can boost self-esteem and resilience.

I think that while dyslexia presents challenges; it is not a barrier to success. By recognising the different ways dyslexia manifests in children and adults, we can tailor our support to meet their unique needs. Those with dyslexia are valuable members of their communities and can succeed with understanding and support.

Effects of Dyslexia

Dyslexia affects the lives of children and adults, affecting daily functioning. Some effects are:

1. Difficulty with reading can affect the grades of a dyslexic. This doesn't mean the person isn't smart; however, as reading plays a huge role in academics, this will harm one's grades.
2. A dyslexic may have low self-esteem. This usually begins in primary school, when a child is teased or scolded by teachers and classmates because of his challenges. He might not consider himself intelligent enough or might believe he's inferior to others.
3. Avoid public speaking. Fear of public speaking comes with dyslexia. We worry we will make a mistake or just freeze. Dyslexia restricts the

easy flow of words, as dyslexics have to take time to understand letters and words.

4. Could be depressed because of frustration. Lagging behind can be disheartening, potentially causing depression. The challenges of reading and writing can be upsetting for people with undiagnosed dyslexia.

5. May be wildly disorderly or compulsively orderly. Being chaotic might develop when a dyslexic tries to complete a task within a short time. A dyslexic realising that time is important may be meticulously orderly, planning ahead and putting everything in place, so that things will go according to plan and on time.

6. May have a poor handwriting in order to mask wrong spellings. I remember my school notes filled with poor writing, with most of my

classmates unable to read them. To catch up with the pace of the teacher, I had to write spellings that came to my mind. It wasn't until classes were finished that I realised many mistakes had been made when going over my notes.

7. Dyslexic children usually do well in sports, arts, or music – since reading is a task to them, they may find other outlets to express themselves. Such areas do not seem challenging as learning how to read.

8. Distracted. When something seems difficult, we find other activities to turn our attention to. Children are distracted and a dyslexic is even more so. A butterfly trapped in the window may seem more interesting to a child than reading a passage, because he knows reading is no fun and is difficult.

9. May thrive in careers where visual talents can be realised. Such careers include carpentry, electrical, interior decorating, artisans, acting, music, for example. These are fields where reading and writing are not integral.
10. May have difficulty excelling in the workplace, especially where reading and writing play a great role. This could be in fields like law, medicine, accounting, history and similar.
11. May be angry and aggressive, especially when the condition is mentioned, or when challenges arise frequently.

Support for dyslexia

Treatment first begins with a diagnosis, to be sure that a person has dyslexia and not another learning disability. A doctor or specialist will have to run some tests to see how well a person reads or writes. This may also involve a psychologist. When the diagnosis is clear, then a learning program can be worked on by the parties involved. Support could be:

1. Reading programmes
2. Special education
3. Educational techniques or strategies
4. Speech therapy
5. Brain training

It is important to note that early detection and evaluation can quickly improve success. Supports are individualised to suit a person's needs.

Chapter Two
My Dyslexia Story

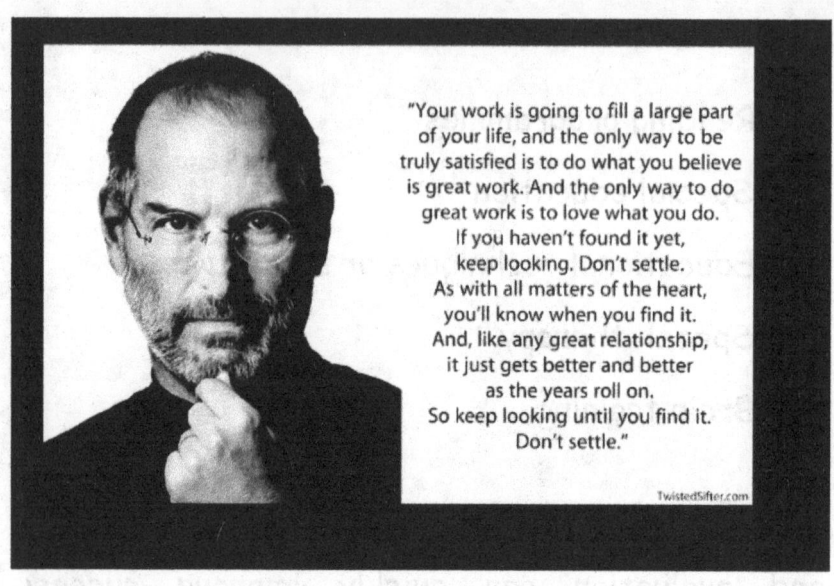

I am writing my story for the second time as this is my first solo book. Telling my story of living with dyslexia is difficult. First, your parents might deal with the guilt that they are in some way responsible for your struggles, and then you have to deal with the same guilt when you have your children, recognising the struggles your child may experience. I discovered this first-hand.

I grew up in a French-speaking city in Douala, Cameroon. I was an outgoing child – I played like most children my age did but uniquely quiet, I will not speak unless spoken to. But when it was time for academics, I had difficulties. It was like there was another side of me. One moment I was happy playing, and the next, when it came to settling down to a book, I went cold and felt sleepy.

My parents knew something was amiss, and initially, they moved me from one school to another, hoping that I would fit in and develop just like most of my age mates. As parents, you have intuitions about your child, and they believed I would learn better in a small class. Despite their efforts, they did not know the true cause of my challenges in reading and writing, so they were working blindly in their efforts to help me. Now that I am a parent, I understand how frustrating it must have been for them not to know why I struggled with what seemed so simple to many.

Throughout my primary and secondary school years, I went to summer school. I also got moved to a small village school where the students in my class were fewer. My parents believed a smaller class would help develop my reading and writing skills. While my performance improved, I still struggled with spelling and had great difficulty taking notes. I would write for ten minutes, then my hand would get cramps, and my attention would wander. No matter how much I tried, I was always behind the other students and this frustrated me.

It became worse in secondary school. Notes were dictated by teachers, and we, the students, had to be fast and write with precision and accuracy. It was rare for any teacher to write on the board. While I wasn't the only who couldn't keep up with the teacher's speed, other students often caught up with help from their peers during breaks – it was this stage I realised my situation was not unique, that I wasn't alone. But for me, I still had difficulties and I went home with empty spaces in my notes. Most times, I had to borrow notes home or fill in the blank spaces with my own thoughts, which itself was a recipe for failure.

However, I struggled to keep up and worked harder. – this resulted me copying my classmates' notes into the night or asking classmates to help me write as well. My efforts helped as in the classroom I did well, and I was pleased that I had caught up. However, when the exam results always came, I was disappointed, and so were my parents. I always received average marks on exams, despite my efforts. This was very frustrating for me. It seemed like my efforts were all in vain.

My biology teacher, Mr. Daniel, was a great help to me, and I am grateful to him. I don't know what he saw in me, but he believed in me. He would meet with me to show me why my performance was average. He implied familiarity with the answers, noting recurring spelling mistakes.

I developed a self-mechanism to hide my struggles – I did not overcome or cure the dyslexia; Most times I pretended I was in tune with the rest of the class if we were reading a passage in a book. Meanwhile, I did not know what was happening – in my spare time; I read at my own pace. When teachers dictated, I scribbled away, writing whatever came to my mind, and made up for it later. This still affected my grades, but at least I didn't get called out in class for lagging. It wasn't until later that I understood how common it is for dyslexic kids to hide their reading and writing difficulties in traditional schools. Children don't want to be embarrassed by their teachers; they don't want to be singled out; and most of all, they don't want to be teased by their classmates for being different.

Years later, while I was at the university studying nursing, I came across the word dyslexia and its characteristics. I had heard this word in passing but never took an interest in it until now. It was at this point things made sense. One thing I noticed was that slow speech in children can be a sign of dyslexia. Another point was that dyslexia can be hereditary. I recalled my difficulties and my three-year-old child's slow speech development. My son's struggles had concerned me, but I dismissed them as temporary; his difficulties mirroring mine never crossed my mind until that moment.

In fact, I had struggled in the UK for my child to get support with his academic work. I was met with responses like, "Your child is too clever to be struggling." It seemed like history was repeating itself with what my parents had been told. I had never made the connection until then. Then, fear gripped me. If I had dyslexia, there was a huge possibility my child did, too. I knew what I went through as a child and what I still experienced as an adult. I didn't want that for my little boy. But to be sure, I needed to get tested.

The test results showed that I indeed had dyslexia. Knowing the truth scared me even more. I was concerned about my son. However, it gave me great comfort, especially when I did more research. I realised it had never been my fault having difficulties and I was proud of myself for excelling despite the struggles. I was also happy that I knew better; my parents had not had the knowledge to truly help me, but I was armed to help my son.

For the time being, I kept the finding to myself and continued to learn more. It is with a deep sense of fulfilment that I put this aspect of my life into this book. To help guide other families with learning needs, we went to court, got justice, a EHCP and part funding for his education.

For more information on achieving your goals despite having dyslexia, visit **www.dyslexiawithsuccessbook.com**.

Chapter Three
The Survival of a Dyslexic Nurse

Imagine a dyslexic from london meeting the queen of England. It's mind-boggling stuff, but that shows how much potential you have.

DR EBUNOLUWA MAGGIE ADERIN-POCOCK

During the writing of this chapter, my impression was that I was the sole African ethnic minority woman living in the UK with Dyslexia. Then I heard of Dr Aderin- Pocock, who spoke openly about her struggles with dyslexia and her achievements. As I stepped into the world of nursing sharing my reality I begin to wonder how many people are like me as a nurse, struggling in silence with aim just to get by as a breadwinner, I didn't realise I would be stepping into a battlefield, a war where my biggest enemy was my own brain. Dyslexia, a term that once seemed distant and abstract, had now become the shadow I could never shake. It impacted every part of my life, from the moment I stepped onto the work on ward, I prayed for safety and wisdom, to the long hours after I left. But here's the thing, I was determined to win. I can confidently say I found a way to overcome dyslexia after a long battle.

I had always known that reading and writing weren't my strong suits. At school, I'd struggled to keep up with lessons, falling behind as the other children excelled. I didn't know why. Words seemed to dance on the page and sentences understandable to everyone else presented themselves as puzzles to me, when I was at middle school. But even though I struggled, I was not stubborn, believed in myself. At university there was a lot of support which I used to succeed. There were things I was good at, like numbers and using my hands. I never wanted to be seen as "different" or "weaker." I wanted to succeed. This meant I worked three times harder. I wanted to help people. That dream led me to nursing, but once I started, I realised just how much dyslexia would affect my work. I got diagnose first year at the university when I was doing the children module on child development and I was very keen to get answers to explain why my child could not talk at the age of three years. This led to me discovering I was dyslexic from student support at university.

The First Shift cardiac critical care unit.

I remember my first day as an intensive care nurse like it was yesterday. The hum of machines, the sterile smell of disinfectant, and the quiet bustle of a ward in full swing. It was overwhelming. I was the new nurse on the block, and I knew I had something to prove. I'll succeed in proving I'm not a failure to my kids and colleagues. More importantly, had some support from the university as a student nurse.

As I walked through the ICU, I noticed how quickly everyone seemed to move. Nurses scurried from one patient to the next, inputting data into electronic systems with lightning speed. Doctors rattled off instructions, and it appeared like everyone around me was speaking a language I didn't understand; that is when I devised a method to master everything, by writing everything down and not talking much so I don't lose my train of thought at work. While my brain processed information differently, I enhanced my visual skills with the patient in front of me. I would start from the head working my way down to the toe, in a systematic way, keeping good view of the ventilated patient pasture in my mind, I watched my colleagues scribble down notes, make rapid decisions, I learnt faster observing from repetitive of nursing routine, I will check and double check things, after some time I catch up with my colleagues who would glide through their rounds like it was second nature.

For me, every note was a mountain to climb. The nights were my worst enemy. Scribbles of numbers and abbreviations that looked like a foreign language, but I learned by making extra notes in my handbook. I'd stare at the monitors, the ventilators, the drip feeds, and try to make sense of the blinking lights and beeping sounds. My colleagues seemed to understand instinctively what to do when the machines beeped, but I needed time sometime and double body to process things, it was good because critical care you work in pairs you check one nurse medication they will check your too, my focus was only on one patient which worked well for me to develop quicker. In a world where split-second decisions could mean the difference between life and death, time was a luxury I didn't have. But I could not work on the ward with five to ten patients needing your attention and staff to manage.

I learned quickly that critical care nursing wasn't just about treating patients. It was about absorbing and synthesising information in real-time. But with my dyslexia, that real-time often seemed like lack time. Instructions that were delivered quickly sometimes got jumbled in my mind. I'd look at patient records after a night shift. I would get brain freeze trying to find the right word. Even worse, in trying to figure out what I had written earlier in a rush after night shift, my dyslexia had the better of me. During the day shift was much faster and more efficient and sorted my job. I learnt I was not a good night nurse and a great day nurse.

The Power of Focus

One thing I realised early on was that I couldn't rely on the same methods as my colleagues. While they could multitask with ease, I had to be laser focused. I couldn't afford distractions, and I couldn't let my mind wander. They thought I was unfriendly and took life too seriously. It wasn't that I didn't know what to do; it was that my brain needed a different approach to get the job done right.

I developed a system. My superpower to hyperfocus saved the day. A method that allowed me to operate within my limitations and still provide top-notch care. Whenever I had to administer medication, I followed a rigid routine. I would triple-check everything. First, I'd read the label, then I'd double-check it before preparing the dosage, and finally, I'd check one last time before administering it to the patient. To an outsider, it might have seemed excessive, paranoid even. But for me, it was a fight for survival. It was the only way I knew how to ensure I didn't make a mistake.

I couldn't afford to rush. In intensive care, one wrong dosage, one missed note, one delayed decision could cost someone their life. And I was terrified of that responsibility. My intention was to help people. Every shift, the weight of my dyslexia pressed on my shoulders. It whispered doubts into my ear, *what if you get it wrong? What if you miss something?*

But then I realised something; dyslexia wasn't just a limitation. It also offered an advantage. Where others moved fast, sometimes without thinking, I moved with care. I took my time. I double-checked, then triple-checked, and I made sure everything I did was done correctly. I wasn't the fastest nurse on the ward, but I was the most thorough.

Seeing the World Differently

One of the most unexpected gifts dyslexia gave me was the ability to see things from a different perspective. My brain didn't process information like everyone else's, but that also meant I noticed things others didn't. I was good at spotting small details in patients' conditions, test results, smells and behaviour.

It was as if my brain was wired to look for patterns and outliers, and I became skilled at reading between the lines. Sometimes, this meant catching early signs of deterioration that others missed. I might not have been able to process words on a page as quickly as my colleagues, but I could spot a patient's discomfort or distress before anyone else. I became attuned to the small things. Things that, in intensive care, made all the difference.

For example, I remember a night shift when I was assigned to a patient recovering from heart surgery. The numbers on the monitor were fine, the vitals were stable, but something about the patient's breathing pattern nagged at me. It wasn't anything drastic, just a subtle irregularity that seemed off. I called the doctor over, but the readings showed nothing alarming. Still, I trusted my gut and insisted something wasn't right.

Later that night, the patient had a sudden cardiac event. We were able to respond quickly, and he survived. The doctor later admitted that without my early intervention, things could have gone much worse. These moments confirmed my progress despite hardship.

The Struggle with Words

As a dyslexic, words have always been my greatest challenge. Whether reading or writing, I constantly battled with letters and words moving on the page or missing and sentences that seemed determined to evade me. In nursing, this meant that documentation was a constant source of stress. Patient notes needed to be accurate, detailed, and timely. But for me, writing them was like wading through quicksand.

I developed strategies to cope. I used abbreviations and bullet points wherever I could. I tried to focus on key information, vitals, medications, and observations. I kept things simple, knowing that if I tried to write too much, I'd get lost in my own sentences. My notes occasionally fell short of expressing my ideas completely. I worried my colleagues would think I was lazy or careless because my notes weren't as detailed as theirs.

But I learned I could compensate in other ways. I became a more verbal communicator. plan I made a point to talk through patient care with my colleagues during handovers, in addition to written notes. I explained my observations, my concerns, and my reasoning out verbally. It was a perfect solution, and it allowed me to share the important details that my notes sometimes lacked.

Working with Patients and Families

Another challenge I faced as a dyslexic nurse was communication with patients and their families. I've always struggled to find the right words in high-pressure situations. When families were upset or anxious, I often fumbled for the right thing to say. Emotions would well up inside me, but they'd get stuck somewhere between my brain and my mouth.

Sometimes I believed I was letting them down. Nursing involves providing comfort and reassurance alongside medical care, especially during challenging times. But I worried that my inability to express myself properly was letting them down.

Over time, I learned to let my actions speak for me. I was able to diver eloquent comfort words, but I could also hold hands, give a smile of hope, or sit with a patient with patience at a much-needed company. I might not deliver eloquent speeches, but I could hold a hand, offer a smile, or sit with a patient who needed company. I found that sometimes, silence was enough. The families appreciated the care I gave to their loved ones, even if I couldn't always find the words they wanted to hear to explain it.

I also developed stronger listening skills. When I couldn't think of the right thing to say, I focused on being a good listener. I let families talk through their worries, their fears, and their hopes.

And even if I couldn't respond perfectly, they knew I was there for them. They knew I cared.

Finding My Place in Intensive Care

Despite all the challenges, I found my home in the ICU. In a strange way, critical care nursing suited my dyslexic brain. It was a field where attention to detail mattered more than speed. Meticulous care could mean the difference between life and death. The slower pace of caring for one or two patients at a time allowed me to practice my methods of checking and rechecking without feeling rushed.

Intensive care became my sanctuary place where I could be the best nurse, I knew how to be, there was a lot of analysis and critical think which I was good at, I had undivided attention on one patient; It was very interesting and visual for me looking at the anatomy from head to toe; it was like mind mapping the connects of one body systems to the other as the wires run by the bed across the patient's chest, mouth and neck or groin, which even with my learning differences. I developed a reputation for being cautious, thorough, and attentive to my patients. I might have taken longer than some of my colleagues to complete my tasks, but I never compromised on the quality of care I delivered.

Looking back, I realise that my dyslexia wasn't a barrier to being a good nurse; it was a different way of being a nurse. My dyslexia forced me to be more thoughtful, more deliberate, and more careful in everything I did. One effect of dyslexia is that it affects your interaction with others. Reading and writing make up a huge part of our daily lives. They translate into speaking, which is the major means of communication. As a dyslexic, having a job that requires constant human interaction can be a struggle. This is why most dyslexics are introverted and have quiet jobs which do not require interactions.

Nursing requires interacting with patients and other medical professionals. It seemed like the worst place for a dyslexic like me. However, prior to my diagnosis and even now, I love being a nurse but my disability never restrained me from reaching my potential.

As a nurse, I care deeply but struggle to communicate my feelings effectively. This makes communicating with the families of patients difficult, as I didn't always have the right words to. I was too worried to say the wrong things being self-aware. There are many times I go quiet or visualise a few words in my mind, and there have been times I have been misunderstand my decisions made for patients. However, I have always had their best interests at heart.

Notes are important in the medical field. We look at them all the time and this way we get to keep tabs on patients. Notes are also shared with colleagues to keep them abreast. My notes were short and informative enough at times, as I would love them to be. I couldn't find the right phrases I wanted to use because of my spelling inability. The times I get to share my notes with others; I see the confusion on their faces as they are illegible dysgraphia and cannot be understood by others but me.

Lacking an editor to review my notes for spelling errors, I anxiously feared overlooking patient details. This also causes a bit of anxiety not to make any spelling errors, so I take twice as long as my colleagues to read my notes over.

This has also affected me in making reports, as I take a very long time to document even minor details because I want them to be perfect.

The need to avoid omissions, spelling errors increases my task completion time. I have to read instructions more than once before I understand them and this can be quite embarrassing.

Every step of the way, when completing a task, I have to look over my notes to ensure that I am doing things right. Being observed made me feel anxious; I feared errors or a lack of trust.

It's not easy to be a dyslexic nurse; the job was high pressure, and dyslexia multiplies that pressure immensely. Nursing is rewarding yet frustrating due to the fast pace and volume of paperwork and instructions. A divine calling led me to nursing, but the immense pressure was disheartening. These were the days when my disability got the best of me.

This book is the first time I have talked about this aspect of my life, about how my disability affects my profession. It's a subject I've always been insecure about. But writing these words has brought calm and healing to me. And I know it will bring healing to other nurses who struggle with this dyslexia in the medical profession.

Working as an agency nurse to make more money was the most stressful challenge I had as a dyslexic. I came to realise that dyslexics don't perform well under stress. It is like a ticking bomb because dyslexics need to be patient, they strive in a controlled and calm environment. I was also scared of the unknown, which intensified my stress. My agency job demanded quick learning and adaptability. This was incredibly stressful but at the same time easy. Also, I had a picture in mind, I went to the same hospital for ease of the job. At that time in my life, and as much as I tried to hide it, my dyslexia kept on rearing its head. I would trip and almost fall on flat surfaces without obstacles on a busy day from running around the ward.

I did my best to hide my challenges from staff and patients by working differently from others. I tried to do things patiently and slowly, but in a hospital things are usually in a rush, and it was in these moments my struggles became clear. I struggled with anxiety, sweating, and lost maximinum productivity under pressure or when dealing with urgent requests.

After multiple research and extensive reading, I realised that zoning out when there was an emergency was because my brain did not have enough time to process information and I was trying to cope in a new environment. My brain was dealing with multiple information, and this affected my limb coordination, which to the brain was not a simple task. After years I discovered I had little bits of the different forms of dyslexia.

Over time, I have worked on safety and success management methods that have helped me as a nurse. These methods include:

- When writing notes, write out key points.
- I dedicate and focus my attention on what I am doing to avoid errors. I get distracted and let my mind trail, but in order to stop this, I focus on the moment.

- I first check the labels of medication immediately I get it out of the medication cupboard. I check it again before preparing it. Then I check it for the third time before administering it. There are a lot of checks but this way I don't make errors.
- If an IV medication is involved, I check it four times. Being careful and constantly checking are procedures of medication administration but I go the extra mile because of my learning needs. I would say this made me more conscious and careful with my work. It takes longer than usual compared to others but I prefer to be slow or to take longer than to be sorry.
- I have noticed that it is only in the critical care environment that I have enough time for me to have this intensive, vigorous,

examination and cross-checking of my work in other not to make any mistakes. This is why I resulted to specialise in critical care nursing – in other areas with the rush and suddenness I would not be so lucky to plan and exert my methods carefully. This area gives me enough time to practise and deliver safe care to my patients. As a critical care nurse, I care for a maximum of two patients at any time, which gives me enough time to ensure patient well-being. I have always practised as a nurse without support from my employer and this sector of nursing gave me the opportunity and plenty of time to support my work and colleagues with no extra help. I've always feared judgment regarding my learning needs. I could be treated differently and this is not something I want.

- Emergencies and interruptions occasionally disrupt my measured work, hindering my ability to fulfil my duties satisfactorily. I still try to carry out my duties notwithstanding so as not to come out as rude or incompetent.
- The difference between working on the ward and intensive care is that I work with more patients, about four. In the ward, there is more information overload for me to handle. Sometimes there's less nursing work on the ward but there is more social interaction, which I struggle with – there are just too many people talking at the same time.

In order to survive as a registered nurse, I have a system:
- I write everything I am supposed to do in a checklist so I don't forget.

- I have to tell my brain that I don't need to talk too much. So, most times I keep quiet and only talk when I am addressed. This might seem rude, but engaging in talks distracts me and makes me forget the tasks I am supposed to do.

- I work in a systematic order that differs from the way others operate. I focus on one task at a time and move on to the next when I am done. When I am given a task, I decide on how long it will take and just get right into completing it. Removing every other thing from my frame of thoughts.

- I focus on the quality of the job I need to deliver. It might seem like a great idea to just get it over with, but quality care for my patients is important. As an agency nurse, I found out that we can get caught up in delivering quality care and creating a nurse-patient relationship. Most times, one of the two often suffers. I am polite to my patients but I concentrate on quality care.

- I overcompensate for my dyslexia by working harder in unaffected areas. This way I balance my efforts so I will get no complaints.

- I discovered I am good at manual and physical work like washing the patients, making beds, taking patients for walks and to procedures, transferring and feeding patients, repositioning patients, changing the wound dressing, and giving medication on time. So, I do these more.

To work at the heart of a sensitive field like nursing presents challenges to anyone, particularly those with learning disabilities, but the proper techniques and patience allow for success and personal development. This was my story and know better through self-education. Better systems and support to be a high functioning adult and focus on things I do best.

Chapter Four
Guide to Managing Dyslexia

Despite having no cure, dyslexia is a learning disability you can manage and control to live a great life. Managing dyslexia is not a walk in the park. It can take years to get it right and to get things under control. It is also a lifelong journey.

Living and working with dyslexia

Dyslexia is bound to show in different areas of your life, especially in your place of work. You can manage dyslexia at home and in the workplace by:

- Let your family, friends, co-workers and superiors be aware of your disability: The reason I have told no one at work about my disability is that I don't want to be looked at with pity or treated differently, but depending on your work environment, you might get a different reaction. Many countries have laws to prevent workplace discrimination against people with learning difficulties.

- Plan your words: Different occupations require different vocabularies. In law, legal terminology such as plaintiff, defendant, and damages is usually used. This is different in the medical field. Find a program or an app to help you reinforce these words.

- Plan for extra time: Time is a major factor at work. As a medical professional, time is very important. Because of your disability, you will need to allocate extra hours for tasks that may take longer to complete.

- Stay organised: Stress affects everyone in the workplace but it can be devastating if you are already struggling with a learning difficulty. To avoid feeling overwhelmed, stay organised and manage your tasks effectively.

Help available for employees with disabilities DWP.

The Department of Work and Pensions (DWP) protects people with disabilities, including dyslexics. You could access the Disability Living Allowance, which is not taxed. It also regulates that employers should make work conducive for those with disabilities. Visit https://www.gov.uk/browse/disabilities

Educational system support for students and parents

By law, publicly funded schools and local authorities must try to identify and help assess children suspected of having dyslexia. There are several support systems to help parents and students in managing dyslexia. These programs provide information to parents and teachers. They include: The British Dyslexia Association, Department for Education, Dyslexia Action, and The Dyslexia-SpLD Trust.

What is the difference between illiteracy and dyslexia?

People with dyslexia are not illiterate. They can read and write, although they have difficulty doing so. Illiteracy is the inability to read or write.

Proper support prevents dyslexia from causing illiteracy.

How do I know I have dyslexia?

Difficulty reading and writing is a sign that you may have dyslexia. You may also exhibit some symptoms mentioned in the chapters above. However, to be sure, take a test with a psychologist.

When do I test for dyslexia?

Dyslexia is overlooked and may be blamed on several factors. Childhood dyslexia testing allows for timely adult interventions. However, anyone can always get tested. There is no single test for dyslexia and tests may encompass questionnaires, vision, hearing, and brain tests, medical, and family history, reading and psychological tests.

Why do you have to test for dyslexia?

Symptoms of dyslexia are like ADHD, difficulty with memory, and dyscalculia. While a dyslexic may also suffer from other learning disabilities, to follow through with the right supports, a test is required.

Chapter Five
Guide for Parents

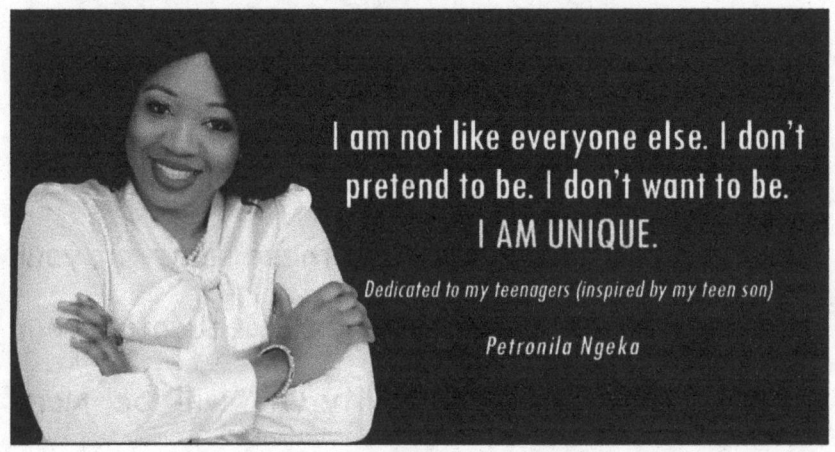

As a parent of a dyslexic child, you play an important role in the life of your child. I acknowledge the guilt you may sense about your child's difficulties, and I had to deal with this first. However, I have to understand that I am not responsible, and I should also not fault my parents. Dyslexia is one of those genetic factors many are not aware of. However, your being aware is the first step towards ensuring your child has a better life.

I remember how frustrating it was for me to be behind my classmates because of my difficulties, and your child might assume an introverted nature or low self-esteem. You, as a parent, need to watch out for these signs, sit your child down and talk to him or her. By educating your child about his/her disability, he will be more prepared for the challenges. He/she will know they are not alone, as there is a supportive community.

You will have to battle ignorant teachers who don't possess the knowledge about dyslexia. To protect your child, you need to make a real effort to learn, read, and connect with other parents.

It can be a tiring journey, but you and your child will emerge happy and strong. If you suspect your child has dyslexia, a diagnosis is important to be sure, and then you will know the steps to take.

    Your child looks up to you as a guidance, and in this time of difficulty, you need to be his/her light of hope. Despite over 60 years of dyslexia research in the UK, my child did not receive proper support until I challenged my local authorities for systemic failures—including a doctor issuing a report about seeing my son, even though we missed the appointment due to the COVID-19 lockdown. I went to court spent over 17 thousand pounds for justice for my child to prevail and we were issued an Educational, health care plan. sometime as a parent you have to go private to get the right support as resource might be limited, My son did 6 years in private school and we had 2.5 years of partial funding to cover the special needs elements of his education. You are not alone in this journey there many parents going through similar challenges as I learnt from my son's school. Positive approach will help you be that system you children need outside all the other parental roles.

Chapter Six
What can be done to embrace dyslexia?

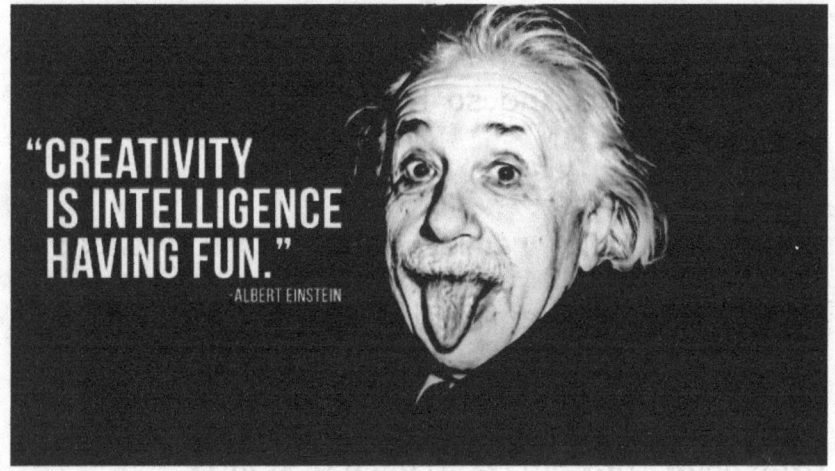

Dyslexia is a disability that comes with discrimination in school and the workplace. It also comes with being bullied or laughed at, especially in schools.

There is a lot of misunderstanding about dyslexia in the society. Some mistake dyslexia for illiteracy. Some think dyslexics are idiots.

Teachers call out dyslexics for assimilating slower than others. While many think dyslexia is just an excuse for not doing well in school or work.

Many have lost their jobs because of the challenges that come with dyslexia. Relationships have suffered. And so has the mental health of dyslexics.

Many don't realise how diverse dyslexia is and the powerful effect it has on those living with the disability. A huge percentage of dyslexics don't even know they suffer from a disability.

These and many other forms of discrimination have led to fear, anxiety, and shame in many dyslexics. Discrimination makes reading and writing even harder.

The first step towards embracing dyslexia is creating awareness. People need to be aware of the dynamics of dyslexia so they can understand it.

When people are equipped with knowledge, the world may be a better place for dyslexics. They will lend a helping hand when people identify as dyslexic.

Awareness needs to be spread in schools. Teachers and students need to notice dyslexia to curb the bullying that most dyslexics face in secondary institutions. This will also equip the teacher with the right ability to educate dyslexics, who learn at a slower pace.

It begins with local awareness (schools, communities) and grows into global understanding.

Social media has proved itself to be a great tool of dissemination. Almost everyone is on their phone nowadays. With social media, people around the world can be educated on dyslexia, and learn to accept and manage it.

Seminars, TV shows and programmes, books, and debate, are also ways awareness can be created about dyslexia.

With awareness, there should be adequate institutions dyslexics can reach out to for help. Such institutions include the British Dyslexia Institute. Dyslexic individuals and their families need accessible information and support from relevant organisations. This will help people understand benefits, education resources, and dyslexia testing.

Perhaps the most powerful step in accepting dyslexia is acceptance. You accept that you have a disability. People around you, like your family, friends, co-workers and superiors, need to accept this as well. Accepting your neurodiversity means understanding that it's not your fault, your parents' fault, or your child's fault. Acceptance is a tough process, but it is important to embrace who you are and forge on to a better life.

Embracing Neurodiversity and Dyslexia - A Call for Change letter.

Dear Non-Dyslexic Community,

I hope this letter finds you well and in good spirits. Please take a moment to understand and appreciate the beauty of neurodiversity within the dyslexia community. I ask for your patience and open-mindedness as you read these words. For they hold the voices of many people who struggle to express themselves in the face of unique challenges.

We must recognise and support neurodiverse individuals facing communication challenges. People with dyslexia, despite their struggles, possess incredible intelligence, compassion, and a strong willingness to enrich society. They yearn for your support and understanding to lead fulfilling lives and share in the joys of existence alongside their fellow human beings, within their communities, church, and families.

If you have a family member or know someone with dyslexia, you might have noticed how they excel in certain areas while facing challenges in others. It is crucial to acknowledge that within a family, we all possess unique abilities. Some people may excel in their studies but struggle with hands-on tasks or following directions, showing traits of dyspraxia. As parents, siblings, or relatives, let us be supportive and encouraging, guiding them to explore their strengths and abilities.

For far too long, many dyslexic individuals have remained undiagnosed and unsupported. By reading this letter, you are already taking a step towards raising awareness and reducing the stigma attached to dyslexia. Let us embrace the fact that we are all different, each with our own set of talents and limitations. Reject labels and stereotypes; embrace our community's vibrant diversity.

In the workplace, dyslexic people often face misconceptions, being labelled as slow, lazy, or unable to cope. People with dyslexia are misjudged by some employers and colleagues who don't understand their abilities. We must come together as a community and work towards creating inclusive environments that value and nurture the strengths of all people. In our churches, schools, sport, and workplaces, regardless of their learning differences.

People with dyslexia possess exceptional gifts that enrich our society. Dyslexic people have succeeded in many fields, using their creativity and analytical skills. Many successful people, including actors, artists, and entrepreneurs, have dyslexia, showing that dyslexia doesn't limit success.

As I bring this letter to a close, I request you to spare some time to reflect on the statistics and evidence that show the number of undiagnosed dyslexic children and adults in our community. Shockingly, one in four people may experience dyslexia in some capacity today. Together, we can work towards early identification, proper support, and the creation of a more inclusive society for all.

Let us be the change we wish to see by being a "dyslexia friend" as we celebrate dyslexia week once a year in October. Embrace neurodiversity at its finest and celebrate the uniqueness that each individual brings to the table. By doing so, we can create a world where everyone's abilities are recognised, valued, and uplifted.

Thank you for taking the time to read this letter, and may it inspire you to be part of the positive change we seek.

With heartfelt gratitude,

Petronila Ngeka,

Author & founder Cameroon dyslexia association

Admin@cameroondyslexiaassociation.org

Chapter Seven
Prejudice
of Dyslexia

In developed countries like the United Kingdom, to an extent there is a lot of information and institutions put in place geared towards disabilities. Also, laws are regulated to protect people with disabilities. Therefore, people like me, who live with dyslexia, can enjoy certain benefits. Developed countries fund disability research through various sources, including governments, schools, charities, and individuals.

However, in less developed countries, things are different. With a lack of funds, manpower, awareness and ignorance, people living with disabilities suffer a great deal. A huge percentage of people in less developed countries are not aware of dyslexia. When a child has issues reading and writing, such a child is called names such as idiot, blockhead, stupid, slow, and other foul words by parents, teachers, and classmates. Worse, some children are caned or punished for their inability to read and write. Institutional prejudice, school will separate children on class put those that excel in one class called class A and those that are below average they call it class B, they will put potential children who will pass GCE in to write internal and those they are unsure of to write externally and they school to score a 100% on public exams to show good performance of the school to the public. No, providing additional or special needs education plans or support to those that are lacking.

Growing up in Cameroon, I was fortunate to have parents who were educated and this meant I wasn't ridiculed for my difficulties. And while some of my teachers were kind and patient, that wasn't always the case. There were times I was perceived as stubborn by teachers because I stopped writing or I had blank notes. There were times I was called names because I had forgotten something that had just been taught. For others, the lingering trauma of ridicule compounded their suffering.

Many Black communities, particularly in developing countries, equate disability with physical impairments. The concept of disabilities being mental or related to reading and writing escapes their minds; Many do not understand that the brain is the engine of the body and that when the brain is wired differently, this can affect a person's performance. So, in such communities, the mention of dyslexia prompts immediate rejection. Parents and teachers will tell you to read more, give you treats or threaten you with punishments. What these causes is fear, and the real problem is never addressed.

    Ameer Baraka is a US author, actor, and a dyslexia advocate. He is a co-founder of the Dyslexia Awareness Foundation. He was 23 and behind bars when he was diagnosed with dyslexia. In school, he had difficulties reading and writing, and was scolded by his teachers and mother, who called him dumb and stupid. In prison, he was able to learn to read and write and send letters to those at home. Today, with the help of his foundation, he reaches out to state correction systems to offer dyslexia screening for inmates.

As I did more research on dyslexia, I found similar stories like Ameer, and there was one thing I noticed. The ignorance in less-developed countries about dyslexia. Many parents don't want to believe that their children have a mental disability. This conjures an image of straitjackets and mental institutions. However, dyslexia is real and it affects many in our community. Therefore, awareness needs to be created so we can stop the prejudice and cruel treatment of dyslexics.

Poverty is an enormous factor in the perception of dyslexia. Poverty and education are closely linked. While a person does not need to be wealthy to be educated, when a family is poor, their children may not have access to adequate educational facilities based on my experience in the UK. And the parents will not have the required education to know that their child has a disability. Parents in poor families are more concerned about providing basic amenities. They hope that their child will be educated and that this will uplift the family status. The last thing they bother about is dyslexia, and when their child has difficulties, their disappointment is usually vocal. They might pull such a child from school in other to save costs.

People from poor homes are also less likely to be tested for dyslexia. Though inexpensive, tests are secondary to necessities like food, clothing, and shelter. A huge percentage, if not all, do not know what dyslexia means. However, people from educated and wealthy homes are likely to suspect dyslexia and get tested because of their access to resources.

Private education is an effective way to manage dyslexia. This does mean your child will go to a private school as a firsthand experience for my child. It means your child has access to a private tutor, a private class or program with other dyslexics in a specialist school like Bredon in Gloucester UK, there have student from primary to high school, all over the world from Asian, Africa, America and Europe. Tewkesbury. This way, they will move at a pace similar to other dyslexics and be surrounded by a support system. Some of these programs may be free, but in less-developed communities, there will be the notion that these programs are paid for. This makes private education seem accessible only to the educated and wealthy.

I remember growing up and my parents did not know that I had dyslexia. This was because they were part of a less-developed community who were not aware of dyslexia. Millions grapple with similar challenges. And I remained ignorant until I studied dyslexia. Then: My eyes opened. I know what it feels like to be ignorant and the frustration that goes with it. Despite my efforts, I felt unproductive and self-critical. However, when I understood my disability, I learned to deal with, and this has made my life better.

Just like most prejudices, it will not be easy getting rid of the bias that follows dyslexia. It will also take time. A lot of awareness needs to be raised in the grassroots areas in many communities where prejudice exists. It is also going to be a joint effort in countries like Cameroon legislations by governments and individuals will have to be put into place to protect dyslexic communities around the globe where the awareness is lacking.

Change will not happen overnight. It will take years, but generations to come will escape prejudice and stigma.

Chapter Eight
Dyslexia is a Gift

This chapter reflects on my dyslexia and its surprising benefits and superpower. The 3D thinking skill, problem-solving skills. With its flaws and difficulties, dyslexia is a gift if you learn to accept and utilise it. Because they have difficulty in reading and writing, dyslexics see the word in a different way than the average person. They convey messages through drawing, painting, music, demonstration or even delve into science equations. I would love to share my interview with you that I had in 2024 with Global women magazine. We dyslexics adapt to these areas and do exceedingly well compared to non-dyslexics in some areas. Dyslexics depend on their reasoning and visual skills more than other people, and this can heighten these skills. When they look at a problem, they are quick to find a solution that others miss. Their level of curiosity is often greater. We think in pictures instead of in words.

If you are dyslexic, you can harness these special abilities and do great work. Before I share another success story

In the interview, Shedding Light on Minds: A Journey of Triumph over Dyslexia

In the bustling world of entrepreneurship, literature, and advocacy, one individual story shines brightly: Petronila Asang Ngeka. Hailing from Cameroon and now a proud resident of the UK, she embodies resilience, innovation, and compassion. A health and social care company CEO, she leads with expertise and inspires hope for those with dyslexia, a challenge she faced and conquered. With determination and new approaches, she's improving lives and changing perceptions of dyslexia. Join us to hear this influential entrepreneur's story of overcoming dyslexia and inspiring others. Can you share a bit about your journey from growing up in Cameroon to becoming a successful entrepreneur and author in the UK?

I struggled to meet the grades required for university in Cameroon after completing my A-levels. I transitioned into nursing because school was challenging for me, and I found myself more inclined towards practical work. I came to the UK in 2004 when there was a shortage of healthcare workers to work as a senior healthcare assistant in Cambridgeshire.

What inspired you to start your own health and social care domiciliary/supported living agency?

"As a single mother following my failed marriage, I discovered that my child had learning needs. In my journey to find resources to support my son, I found a school for children with dyslexia located in the West Midlands. At this point, I had retrained as a nurse and was working in the ICU. However, the schools I found for my son were all private, which meant I had to pay for his education. Consequently, I relocated from Cambridgeshire to Birmingham and started a care business to help finance his private education. It was challenging, but I succeeded, and my son has been attending Bredon School in Gloucester for five years now and has completed his GCSEs and now A level in 2025". I would say being dyslexic was a challenge, but after discovering myself and accepting the daily challenges I faced, I finally gained strength in some abilities as a dyslexic businesswoman and leader today. My dyslexia gift is being an overthinker, and I use it to my advantage. I can foresee problems in my business before they occur. I can read people and sometimes anticipate their next move or response, which often impresses the administrators in my office. From many failures, a kinder, more understanding leadership style emerged in me.

I have been ashamed of my errors as a dyslexic adult. I was invited to share my journey in

BBC Leicester to share my dyslexia story in my book dyslexia with success when an UK PM was shamed for tweeting with spelling errored. This shed light in the challenges. I experience omissions of words.

When I write, sometimes when I speak, or when I read. I struggle to read notes that are written in capital letters. I experience dysgraphia. Spelling poses a significant challenge for me, and letters appear unsteady on a black and white background.

In my childhood in Cameroon, while a student there with dyslexia, I didn't understand my issue. My knowledge never translated into paper; Although I excelled in speaking, it was as though I was stupid and unintelligent. Upon returning to university in Cambridge after having my children and receiving a formal diagnosis of dyslexia. I received support and performed well. As I considered my past, I chose to aid millions of Cameroonian children facing educational hardship, mirroring my own struggles. I aim to increase awareness and reduce stigma about learning disabilities in my African-Caribbean community, internationally.

One of the biggest challenges I faced was when I encountered Cameroonians in Cameroon, who insisted that dyslexia was not real but mainly a concept. I had to persuade them otherwise, providing practical examples from my own experiences and those of my child. Fortunately, I found that some could relate to the struggles faced by dyslexic individuals, particularly those within their own families or communities.

We often receive complaints from parents who report that their children are being insulted by Cameroon teachers because of their learning difficulties, with inadequate support provided. Our team at CaDyAs acted in arranging seminars, inviting teacher participation. The primary goal of these seminars is to raise awareness and plan training to support dyslexic students in the classroom.

The primary target audience of the Cameroon Dyslexia Association is schools. We know schools are key to helping dyslexic students, so we're working with teachers to make classrooms more inclusive.

How do you incorporate your unique brand and professional solutions into your work with dyslexia and entrepreneurship?

My mission is to serve my community through my home-care business, Mcare24 Limited, which offers round-the-clock care services as an employer with disability and caring and supporting people with dyslexia and various neurodiversity challenges is an opportunity to service and restored hope with empathy and compassion. I aim to make Passion London lipstick available to women worldwide as a symbol of resilience. A reminder that wearing lipstick is not just colour but an embodiment of women, their strength and beauty in the face of adversity.

For five years, I've volunteered, providing Christmas meals to 100 women in impoverished areas. I strive to create positive change that transcends geographical boundaries and uplifts people from all walks of life.

How do you balance being a mother, CEO, and advocate for dyslexia awareness? Do you have any tips for others facing similar challenges?

Waking up and succeeding in business are intrinsic to my role as a mother, as they enable me to provide for my kids. Therefore, maintaining a positive mindset is crucial. I believe in the power of positivity and self-belief. Once you embark on a task, trust that God will bring people to support and manifest your vision. It's important to surround ourselves with positive, like-minded people who can uplift and inspire us.

What advice would you give to individuals with dyslexia who are aspiring entrepreneurs or professionals?

I firmly believe that the failures and challenges stemming from dyslexia can serve as a valuable preparation for entrepreneurship. Every setback encountered because of dyslexia should be viewed not as a hindrance, but as a stepping stone towards success in the entrepreneurial journey.

In business, setbacks and failures are inevitable, yet they are often the catalysts for growth and innovation. Dyslexia, instinct, resilience, adaptability, and problem-solving skills or qualities essential for navigating the unpredictable terrain of entrepreneurship. <u>Can you share any upcoming projects or initiatives you are reworking to further your impact on the dyslexia community?</u>

As the founder of the Cameroon Dyslexia Association, I am thrilled to announce that we will launch our inaugural magazine soon. This magazine will raise awareness of dyslexia and provide resources for dyslexic people, their families, and educators. I am incredibly proud of this milestone achievement for the Cameroon Dyslexia Association, and I look forward to our magazine's positive impact on the dyslexia community and beyond". Therefore, we stand out in certain fields. John Lennon, Agatha Christie, Stephen Hawking, Tom Cruise, Justin Timberlake, Will Smith and so many more.

Here are some ways dyslexics utilise their gifts:
- They are more curious than non-dyslexics.
- They are acutely aware of their environment.
- They are intuitive and insightful.
- They think and perceive using all the senses).
- Their imaginations are vivid.

Without parental or educational suppression, these abilities foster high intelligence and creativity.

Advantages of being dyslexic

Being dyslexic can be loving and caring, but like everything that has its disadvantages, being dyslexic has its advantages, some of which are:

- Many of the world's creatives with dyslexia show high levels of creativity. Dyslexics can be exceptionally creative individuals who excel in music and the arts. There's also evidence that dyslexics are more likely to think in images and that the dyslexic brain is skilled in visual processing. Picasso, Roald Dahl, Orlando Bloom, and Whoopie Goldberg are a few creative minds to mention.

- Problem-solving: Dyslexics are known for thinking outside the box. I guess this is because we are determined and despite having difficulties reading and writing; we try to catch up. We solve problems with an unorthodox approach. We also see new ways of completing tasks.
- Observant: We make use of our visuals and capture things around us. Perhaps we assimilate knowledge this way because reading and writing are difficult for us.
- High levels of empathy enable us to read emotions. I can discern when a person is upset and this has helped me with my patients. Many dyslexics possess the ability to read and understand people, and when this skill is utilised, we connect with others.

Chapter Nine
The role parents, teachers play in Dyslexia.

In this chapter, I am going to be addressing parents, teachers, and dyslexics. This is because this learning difficulty revolves around these three people, mostly the dyslexics.

I know what it's like to wish to be included in class, but your difficulty makes it impossible. I understand the experience of working late into the night, yet academic results don't always show one's intelligence. Or to know the answer but cannot express it in the right form. I am dyslexic and I understand the experience.

As a parent, I understand the hardship of watching your child struggle in their studies while classmates excel is not easy. Seeing your child come home unhappy and without complete notes in their books. We shield our children, but dyslexia exposes them to harsh realities.

For a teacher, it may not be easy having a child who is not catching up like the others. Teaching, like all other jobs, is tasking, especially when dealing with several children. However, being a teacher is more than scribbling on the board. As a teacher, you play an important role in a child's life. Your patience and kindness can transform a child's life.

When a child displays certain traits, not being attentive in class, being left behind, unable to read or write, unable to pass an exam realise that something is wrong, and that the child may not be lazy. I know it can be quite tiring going back and forth with a child, but most times, this is not the child's fault. It may just be a learning disability. Parents may reach out to teachers when they are worried about their children. Together, parents and teachers can figure out the problem and find solutions.

First, know as teachers and parents that every child is not the same. Our brains are wired differently. Josh may be a playful child and Jack a quiet child. Our genetics and environment influence us to become the people we are. This is why for every child, even amongst siblings, they have to be treated in different ways. My parents were more patient with me than with my siblings, who were fast readers and writers. It might have been harder for me if my parents had treated all of us the same way.

Having a disability doesn't mean a person is not capable of being successful. Dyslexia comes at different levels. For some it may be mild, and this may affect reading and writing a little bit, perhaps having difficulty with P and B. It could be moderate as well. And in some cases, severe. While reading and writing are important in society, we can also express ourselves in different ways, through music, drawing, painting, science, and other forms.

Dyslexics can shine in different areas notwithstanding their disability, so do not strike a child off too early, or think there's no hope for him or her. This action will harm a child's self-assurance and prevent them from reaching their full potential.

Business.
- Richard Branson is a British business magnate, investor, author and philanthropist. He's also a billionaire. At 16, Richard dropped out of school because he couldn't keep up. His dyslexia was treated as a handicap and his teachers thought he was lazy and dumb. On his last day of school, his headmaster told him he would either end up in prison or a millionaire. Today's he's the founder of Virgin Group with the popular subsidiary Virgin Atlantic.
- Dean Graziosi is a New York Times bestselling author, investor, and

entrepreneur, who has created a multimillion-dollar real estate business. From a poor background, Dean struggled with dyslexia and could not go to college because his parents could not afford it. While in school, he had to do a number of odd jobs. He couldn't read well and was always in a special reading class. He said this made him think he was unintelligent and beneath others. However, Dean loved working on cars, and while his mates were in college, he got into the auto business and with hard work; he was able to build a successful business and get out of poverty.

- Lisa Nichols was told by her speech teacher in school to get a desk job when she grew up and to avoid speaking in public. She has severe dyslexia, and it took a much longer time to learn from others. After a failure, her English teacher told her, "Lisa, you have to be the weakest writer I've ever met in my entire life." Today, not only is Lisa a best-selling author, but she is also a motivational speaker, a millionaire, and CEO of 'Motivating The Masses' a global platform that has reached nearly 30 million people.

Science

- Albert Einstein, who happens to be the most influential physicist of the 20th century, was dyslexic. He didn't start talking until he was four years old. This delayed speech in children is sometimes called the Einstein Syndrome. He also had difficulty reading aloud. He did poorly with schoolwork, especially arithmetic – he worked hard but always came up with the wrong answers. His teacher said nothing good would come of him. He was also quick-tempered, which could be as a result of his frustration. A great scientist, Einstein is famously known for his equation $E = mc2$ and for his discovery of the photoelectric effect, for which he won the Nobel Prize for Physics in 1921.

Art

- Leonardo Da Vinci was dyslexic. With interest in invention, drawing, painting, sculpture, architecture, science, music, engineering, literature, anatomy, astronomy, botany, palaeontology, and cartography, and so much more, he is widely considered one of the greatest painters of all time. An indication of his disability was in his handwriting. He wrote his notes in reverse, mirror image, a trait sometimes shared by other left-handed dyslexic adults. He was also a terrible speller with his notes filled with errors. His famous artworks include Mona Lisa, The Last Supper, St. John the Baptist, and Salvator Mundi, the most expensive painting in the world, worth more than $450.3 million.

Chapter Ten
You are not Alone.

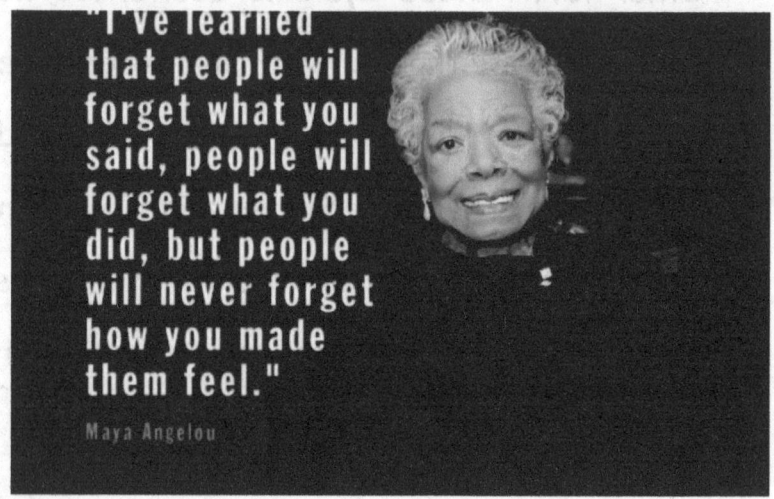

It might not be dyslexia; it might be another disability, but I doubt any human is born abnormal. Our flaws, biologically or otherwise, make us human. We are imperfect.

You could be free from medical issues, then an accident occurs and your life shifts. I witnessed this as a nurse. People who seem to enjoy perfect lives, get their lives altered in just one second.

They didn't see a car coming. It could even be a medical error or a reaction to a drug, and your life changes.

We will always face challenges. It is an integral part of life. No matter how much we try to protect our children, their day at school might be ruined by a bully or when their crush ignores them. As they grow older, they will experience tougher challenges. We may want to take these challenges from them because we believe we are better equipped, but they will learn from these experiences.

For some, it is the loss of a loved one that may change their lives. The pain becomes unforgettable and weighs us down, preventing us from forging ahead in life.

We are unaware of what others endure. I say this for me, and many people who keep their challenges secret. People might see me and go, "Oh! She's a nurse. I want to be just like her." But they don't know how hard it is for me to get through a busy day. That is why I learned to avoid envy as I understand life's challenges. It is also why I treat people with kindness. People face challenging periods daily, and a kind act could brighten their day.

I once came across the story of a man who was going to kill himself when he got home from work. He suffered from anxiety and depression. He made a stop at his favourite cafe to eat one last meal before he ended his life. The waitress left his order with a note. In the note, she said she had missed seeing him around in the past weeks and hoped he was okay. She left an extra doughnut for him, just the way he liked it, warm and full of jam. This act of kindness made him decide not to kill himself and to seek medical help. He had thought he was all alone, that no one cared about him, and that if he died, no one would miss him. To know that someone had been noticing him meant a lot to him in his broken state.

In a world filled with desires to be successful or wealthy, make good grades, make family and parents proud, it can be quite easy to get lost and even selfish that we think of ourselves only. But while we chase after our dreams, we must realise that we are not alone. We might be strong, but there are others who are weak. We might be rich, but there are others who are poor. Even the seemingly strong people need comfort. This is why at times it hits us with shock when a successful person takes their life. We all possess our demons, and as humans, we excel at maintaining a strong facade.

There have been people who have said a harsh word or two because of my challenges. I waved it off, but that didn't mean those words did not affect me. Perhaps it is because I am built with a tough skin, but not everyone is like me. And those words could ruin a person's day and make them unable to function properly.

With an increasing rate of suicides, so many people are fighting silent battles, and a cruel word or action might push them over the edge.

The smallest actions, even a smile, can improve someone's state of mind. Here are some ways we can exhibit kindness to people we come across:

- Compliment a stranger. You will be surprised how this will light up a person's day and keep them smiling whenever they remember your words.

- Hold the door open for the person behind you. You don't have to help with the door only when the person has his/her arms full. It is an act of courtesy and kindness.
- Buy someone coffee. Your colleague or the doorman will be pleased with this act.
- Leave a few nice messages to or even a letter. You can place a sticker with kind words on a car window.
- Buy food, warm clothes, and blankets for someone who is homeless. People fall on hard times and your help might just make their life better.
- Remind people of their worth. You are beautiful. I love your hair. Thanks for doing what you do. These words tend to resonate in weak moments.

- Tip your waitresses/waiters and baristas. They handle nice and rude customers each day, and I'm aware that sometimes they're tempted to quit, but they need the work. By tipping them, you make them realise that you appreciate their efforts.
- Give somebody your seat on the bus. I remember being on a crowded bus after a very long day. I was very tired. I don't know if he saw how stressed I was, but this gentleman offered his seat. It was a huge relief and it made me do some critical thinking on the way home. Don't also forget to thank the bus driver when you get off.
- Donate old clothes and items to charity. Not everyone is as fortunate as you. There are people in need of clothes, books, furniture, etc. Instead of throwing those items away,

donate them to charity and you are bound to make a person's life better. You can even give them to people in the neighbourhood who are in need.

- Appreciate the people who have helped you or made a difference in your life. There are people who have helped you in one way or another. It might have been a teacher in school, the bus driver who let you on when you had no ticket or the doorman who walked you to your door at night. They might have no idea how important their help was. Thank them. This way, they will continue doing good.
- Be extra nice and helpful to someone you know is having a hard time. Some people don't like being the centre of attention. I am one of such. It embarrasses me when people clutter around to help. And I guess this is

why many don't like to share their disabilities with others. While not making it uncomfortable, you can be helpful to someone who is having a hard time. You can pick up a colleague whose car is at the repairs from their home. You can give an envelope of money to a friend who is in need of cash. You can even ensure that the fonts in printouts at the office are large for those suffering from poor eyesight. You don't have to be obvious and let the world know that you are helping, but your acts of kindness will be recognised and appreciated.

- Give somebody a lift home. It could have been a missed bus or no money to get on the train or get a cab. If you see someone in need of a lift and they are headed your way, you could offer them a lift.

You Are Not Alone

As dyslexics, we go through a lot each day. Reading signs, instructions, work notes, and so much more. It can be quite a headache. Your kindness can make a great difference in our lives. How can you be a dyslexic friend?

- Helping with explaining signs and manuals. It can be quite a lot to take in, and it would really be helpful if you could verbally explain the content to us.

- Showing patience towards us. I am one of those people who ensure I get work done no matter how long it will take me. Your being patient gives us the space to do things without mistakes and to produce great results.

- Learn about us. This shows that you care, and you are not just being sympathetic. This also educates you and puts you in a position to educate us. By learning about dyslexia, you can even provide us with helpful information.

By showing an act of kindness to others, you teach them that it is good to be caring, and they will, in turn, replicate the kindness. You never know; you or someone you know might just be a recipient of this cycle of kindness. Showing kindness to others contributes to a better world.

This book, produced during the 2020 coronavirus lockdown, reflects how the pandemic substantially impacted learning requirements across communities, schools, workplaces, and for individuals. As you read this change with the different act of kindness, positivity you give to anybody see as the same kind help you need to give a dyslexic friend or love one

Dyslexia During The Pandemic

During the pandemic, Dyslexia has been more and more prevalent with some of our community members who could be dyslexic, but without them knowing that they have it.

In this chapter, I would be explaining here how dyslexia affects different members of our community, ranging from children, young adults, adults, and members of different ethnic groups in various forms. Some of them who may have been affected with this kind of learning disability could be going on about their daily life activities, with some sort of struggling, but without them knowing that they may have dyslexia.

In bringing Dyslexia understanding to readers, please, I would like you to take a moment and hear my story in this regard.

As the Covid-19 pandemic intensified and the lockdowns in different ways continued on, Many persons and families affected by this form of learning disability were struggling very hard to do the home learning with their children. And this gets even worse, more difficult, and very stressful when parents, guardians and children are affected by dyslexia, like in my own case with my son.

As a dyslexic parent who has been diagnosed with dyslexia. Also, it has been proven with research that dyslexia could be acquired through a hereditary passage from and between family members. Just like in my own case with my child. I have two children; one of them has dyslexia. Both of us, myself and him, struggled with home learning during the pandemic. My child barely gets out of bed and cannot cope with the pressure of online learning.

Although his school provided us with tools and strategies for supporting the schoolchildren with Computers and necessary learning applications. On the merits of the above provisions, one would therefore think that online learning will be a solution for children with dyslexia. However, unfortunately, this was not the case. It is very important to know that the world was trying this form of home learning for the first time. Making it difficult for children with learning needs to apprehend this form of learning smoothly. Therefore, leaving them far too behind to comprehend and adjust. Eventually this form of learning brought lots of stressful moments, confusion, tensions on to the families with learning needs. In most cases to some families, has increased the chances of them (I mean parents and children) developing a mental health burnout and breakdown.

In my household, one of the main issues that we confronted during the pandemic was that the school time coincided with breakfast time. Therefore, we had this huge problem trying to get the children out of bed to have their breakfast in time for them to log into their computers. Although they didn't have to bathe, or dress and go to school. You would think It will be second nature to get out dressed and go and sit in front of the computer. But as we all know, and being human, the mindset and the psychology of children learning at home made them comfortable. They wanted to do their own thing in their home clothes, as their brains did not always or automatically switch to learning modes. **School teachers** delivering lessons online could not notice this from them. When the child was drifting away from learning during the classroom lessons conducted online, distractions from home were a huge contributing factor to children struggling with home Learning. Proven research on Children with dyslexia concluded that they could be more easily distracted from learning than other children without this form of learning disability. Learning from home became more tough for the children affected by dyslexia when the doorbell rang, the washing machine was on, people moved around the house, and the noise coming from outside through the window impacted on children's smooth learning.

What made it really significant for me to share this story with the world and to those who are reading this now is that *I was helpless*. As a student, I didn't like reading and as an adult, I still struggle with. It was difficult for me to support my child with literacy online learning works during the pandemic. There is no doubt that there are people, like me in our wider Community there may be out there many parents and their children, who experienced the same challenges as me in coping with online course work with our children during the pandemic, due to our dyslexic learning needs.

Did you think you did very well and coped at home or did your inability to manage with academic work surface when you were left to support your child with their work?. I am not ashamed to say this. Because. I'm not alone. You are not alone in the struggle of selection with the difference of dyslexia. British Dyslexia association. It is stated that one in five people in the UK is dyslexic. If this is correct. How did we manage to support the people coping with dyslexia in our community during the pandemic, working from home and home learning?

Therefore, as a mother working from home, also dyslexic, I could not cope with this situation and was unable to get support that I highly needed to help my child with his learning needs as I was in the same situation that he was in as well. People who could have assisted me were not available during lockdown. Hence, I struggled to deal with this alone.

My question here to our various Government Institutions such as the Educational Authorities, Local Government Authorities; is are we prepared frow the way we learnt from the pandemic on educational teaching learning as it affects parents and children with learning needs like dyslexia and how to provide those parents and children with adequate supports with the resourced that they would need, to assist their children with their online learning.

For someone like me, I have always had a PA who assists me with my administrative duties.

My ability to recognise omissions in my work; writings, sending and responding to emails and spellings. On the challenges that I faced in these areas.

Of course, I love to write my own emails!! I love being organic and original. Also, some emails that came into my box needed an immediate response. Though I felt very uncomfortable sending it, due to mistakes that I might be making. For me to request somebody else to send them, hence it defeats the timeline when my response to such email would have been replied to.

What I was expressing above was that my inability to respond effectively to those emails promptly was caused by my dyslexia. I found myself using my 12-year-old to proofread the work, to proofread the emails, to identify any mistakes. By omission I put this level of honesty here to encourage other parents and individuals going through the same learning difficulties as myself and my child to come forward so that we could work together to address it, because I know you are not alone. So, look out for my second book. "You are not alone".

I write this last chapter thinking about loneliness; I ask myself, what is loneliness? I begin to wonder and ponder the subject. I don't want to address this from a dictionary point of view but from my observation in the past 19 years working with people. Naively, I used to think loneliness is when you do not have people around you but that is far in between what the world presents to us. I my humble option loneliness is that place where your mind takes you that no one can see or help you unless you tell someone you are in that place where there is no help support with your imagination and physical self, sometimes you struggle to connect the two things. What other people tell me about loneliness is quite different but similar in many ways, because the common thing is the lack.

Loneliness is overcome when you have somebody who believes in you, who can take you to that place where you want to be; you cannot go by yourself. Loneliness is felt in every aspect of life whether you're a mother or father your child, come on brother sister you have family, you have friends; you have a job come on; you have a business come on your manager hundreds of people as employees, in a relationship he will experience loneliness at some point.

It is important to seek help in whichever form is suitable for you keeping in checked with your mental health will avoid you from slipping into love blonde dinners. How much money you have, loneliness cannot go away. All leaders will experience loneliness because you have to be lonely and find a place within yourself where you can discover and create and function at a high level in which you are operating in to achieve exponential success. Loneliness is not always in pain because sometimes when you find it yourself in loneliness, it spurs your imagination and creation. Your mind wants the place that nobody can take you to and nobody can help you unless you ask somebody to come into that place. To come with you, to support you, to enable you and to get you to live life to its optimal state. Sometimes in life we lose people things that we value but it is very important to remember that we cannot lose ourselves. As we talk about loneliness, it is important we also give the reader the opportunity to reflect on themselves and to find out why they are lonely because that is the answer to not being lonely. In my experience of working in health and social care for the past 19 years, so then but they are not lonely. I looked after a 92-year-old lady who lived in a very big house in a small neighbourhood and partial village. Her husband passed away. Her children lived very far away from her. She was always in the reading room and then sometimes she moved into her kitchen, sat there and looked in the garden. I remember asking her this question: "Are you lonely?" She said to me, "You look lonely. I am very happy in my own company and I like it this way. I have done a lot in my life. This time here, I am very pleased. I don't watch TV; I read; I sometimes pray. That is the secret to my life." Some of these encounters, where I thought people were in a very lonely place because they were vulnerable; to support them give them the physical items they need and help them to complete the activities of daily living blinded me to the fact that they may be alone but not lonely. So, I know people who are in their environment alone and not always lonely, but it's always key to discuss the topic. You can be the person that can help somebody who finds themselves in a place where they cannot get out of or need somebody to get them into the place where they are fulfilled and have purpose. Office solitude was never an issue because I always kept busy improving myself to be my best. This phone videos to reach out and impact the community in which you live.

I look at loneliness from the perspective of somebody with a learning disability or learning needs struggling with aspects of life that they think they are the only ones in the world going through this. There are so many people experiencing the inability to read and write still being purposeful, having a dream and a mission to accomplish their goals in life. Residents so it's pinnacle for me to express how I felt when I found myself lonely in the world where I thought I was dumb I was an intelligent because I could not spell, but today in this generation I quickly found out that I cannot be alone and I am not alone because of dyslexia and should not be alone because I cannot spell and haven't got a huge ability to read and write but because there is somebody out there who can take me to where I want to be. Thus, overcoming the loneliness. The invention of audiobooks has created an unparalleled ability for people like me, who find words moving on the page when they read, to stay in the line of reading attacks. I have read more books than I have ever read in my entire life or in the past 35 years when I discovered of course books. Site righted some more when I discovered I don't have to spell all the words correctly because there is the invention of speech notes, dictation electronics,

A story about a lady named Makah, being neurodivergent whether due to her autism, and her sister Lume with ADHD, or her brother Ngwa with dyslexia can be a complex experience. Here's a clearer picture of what someone with ADHD might face, without relying heavily on labels.

When someone with ADHD faces a whole unrestricted day, it can be an overwhelming experience. It's like having a million tasks floating around in their mind, all equally important but impossible to prioritise. Imagine every task, whether it's something as simple as putting away laundry or paying a critical bill, feels like it's vying for attention, like leaves of lettuce tossed around. Important things can get buried in the chaos, and the person might not realise the urgency of one task over another.

Instead of checking off items on a to-do list, there's a lot of wandering, moving things around, and starting projects that never get completed. Outsiders might view this as someone having a leisurely day, but in reality, their mind is buzzing with activity. It's as if all their mental tabs are open at once, flashing non-stop, screaming for attention. There's no true mental wandering; everything is actively vying for space.

This lack of focus often leads to frustration. They might dance or move around to release some of that pent-up energy, only to lose track of what they were supposed to do next. The simple act of completing one task feels like trying to climb a mountain with no clear path. When they do find the motivation, they may forget what they were supposed to do in the first place. Where's the notebook with the to-do list? Oh wait, there are 17 notebooks! And none of them seems to have the list they're looking for, so off to the store they go to buy a new one, starting the cycle again.

ADHD isn't just about distractibility or hyperactivity. In fact, hyperactivity is often internal. It's not about bouncing off the walls; it's about five highly caffeinated squirrels running wild in their head, never slowing down. This constant mental arousal can lead to sleep problems and racing thoughts. The name "Attention Deficit Hyperactivity Disorder" is misleading. What people with ADHD experience isn't a deficit in attention but an inability to regulate it. They can hyper-focus on one task and achieve remarkable things, but only if they're able to engage their mind in the right way.

People with ADHD often have emotional dysregulation, which means their emotions can swing intensely and rapidly. They might excel in high-pressure situations but get overwhelmed by minor issues, or they could overshare at social gatherings and later be anxious, replaying the conversation in their head for months, worrying that others found them "too much."

Paralysis is another challenge. It's not that they don't know what to do, but that the sheer number of tasks can appear insurmountable. Trying to organise those tasks into a priority list can be so overwhelming that they can't even start. Their room might look messy, but they know exactly where everything is because they have a unique system that works for them.

When someone tells them a story, they may reply with their own similar experience, not to shift the conversation but as a way of showing empathy. Despite their capabilities, many struggle with low self-esteem, often stemming from their difficulty in managing everyday tasks. They may become people pleasers to avoid confrontation, leaving them vulnerable to manipulation or abuse. They are also masters of hiding their struggles, leading others to believe they are perfectly fine when, in reality, they are just barely keeping their heads above water.

One of the hardest parts of ADHD is maintaining relationships. Object permanence, typically thought of in terms of physical objects, can apply to people as well. They might genuinely forget to check in with loved ones, not because they don't care, but because those people momentarily vanish from their mental radar. For many neurodiverse people, life often feels like a balancing act, constantly working to stay afloat while juggling a whirlwind of thoughts, emotions, and tasks.

Imagine someone wrapping their arms around a younger version of themselves, reassuring them with a gentle whisper: "You're not broken, just different." This is the message many neurodivergent individuals, especially women with ADHD, need to hear. For so long, ADHD has been misunderstood, particularly in women, where its symptoms are often subtle, masked, or mistaken for something else. Women with ADHD frequently overthink and experience what can be called "intention overload disorder." It's not just about attention deficiency but rather having too many thoughts all at once, all competing for priority.

Picture a stage in an empty room. You sit in the front row, watching as each of your thoughts takes the stage to engage with you. But for someone with ADHD, those thoughts don't exit after the conversation ends. Instead, they linger, while new thoughts enter, and soon the stage is crowded with overlapping dialogues, creating a sense of mental chaos. This constant influx of thoughts can lead to mental exhaustion and difficulty focusing, which is why ADHD can seem overwhelming, not due to a lack of attention, but because of an overload of intention.

For those who don't have ADHD, understanding it can be difficult. Partners and friends of people with ADHD may notice moments where their loved one fixates on a particular detail, hyper-focused to the point where they struggle to move on to new information. This hyperfocus isn't intentional stubbornness or rudeness. It's the ADHD brain's way of processing, and shifting attention can feel like trying to turn a ship around in a storm. The frustration it causes in relationships is understandable, but those with ADHD are often doing their best, even when it seems like they're stuck on a topic or detail.

ADHD is also linked to emotional regulation. What may seem like small frustrations to a neurotypical person can feel emotionally overwhelming to someone with ADHD, leading to arguments or misunderstandings. Afterward, the person with ADHD might replay the conversation over and over, agonizing over what they said, wondering if they came across as too much or if others now think less of them. This is a common cycle for women with ADHD, who may also mask their symptoms, trying to blend in, even when internally they feel like they're drowning in thoughts and emotions.

Neurodivergent people, including those with ADHD, often experience pain differently as well. For some, sensitivity to pain is heightened, meaning that something merely uncomfortable to a neurotypical person might feel excruciating to them. Others might have the opposite experience, feeling little or no pain where others would be in significant discomfort. These differences are not exaggerations; they are real and deeply felt, just like their atypical reactions to emotional or physical pain. For instance, a neurodivergent person might respond physically to emotional pain, feeling a deep pain when their feelings are hurt, or react emotionally to physical pain, like crying when they stub their toe.

Additionally, sensory overload is a common experience for neurodivergent individuals. Bright lights, loud sounds, or certain textures aren't just bothersome; they can be painful. For example, the glare of a light that someone else might find annoying could feel like needles in their eyes. Stress and anxiety only exacerbate these sensitivities, making it even harder to manage daily life.

Neurodivergent individuals often have unique reactions to their environment, like someone with ADHD who spots a deer while berry picking or reacts quickly in a dangerous situation. Their hyperactivity might show up as running around all day without feeling tired or taking risks that others might avoid. They might hear every twig snap in the woods; their senses are finely tuned to their surroundings in ways that can feel overwhelming or exhausting.

For a woman diagnosed with ADHD, simple tasks can take on layers of complexity. She might keep the TV on, not for entertainment, but to feel less alone. She may clean, not because her house is messy, but because her mind is. When she interrupts others mid-sentence, it's not to dominate the conversation, but because she's eager to show that she understands and connects. After social events, she may spend hours or even months worrying that she said too much or that people now see her differently.

Social gatherings can be especially challenging. After oversharing or feeling misunderstood, she might isolate herself, replaying moments from the event in her head, convinced that others found her too intense. When she sees pictures of groups of friends, she may feel a sharp pang of sadness, physically paralyzed by the thought that she isn't truly accepted or understood.

But if she could go back and embrace her younger self, she would whisper, "You are enough. You are not broken." ADHD doesn't define her entirely; it's just part of her story. She would remind her younger self that what she's experienced is real, that her mind works differently, and that she doesn't have to fit into neurotypical expectations to be worthy. Over time, she'll learn to differentiate between what's truly her and what's the mask she wears to cope.

Ultimately, understanding ADHD in women and neurodivergence in general requires compassion. Neurodivergent individuals often feel like they're treading water, trying to stay afloat in a world that moves differently from how their brains work. They are doing their best to navigate a reality where tasks, thoughts, and emotions often feel overwhelming. But with support and understanding, they can thrive, embracing their differences and finding their own unique strengths.

I would like to take a moment to address something important regarding our neurodivergent members, including those with ADHD and autism. Many of them face unique challenges in social situations that might not always be immediately visible, and I believe it's important for all of us to understand how we can better support them.

1. Respect Their Need for Space and Processing Time
When someone becomes overwhelmed in a social setting or reacts strongly to sudden changes in plans, it's not personal. They might need time alone to process what's happening. Instead of asking many questions or feeling hurt by their reactions, give them the space to gather themselves.

2. Be a Safe and Non-Judgmental Presence.
Neurodivergent people often hide their differences to blend in with neurotypical society. Support your friends, regardless of whether they have ADHD or autism, by allowing them to be themselves. Offer them a judgment-free space

where they don't feel pressured to always present themselves as organised or punctual. If someone enjoys repeating certain activities (e.g., watching the same movie multiple times), it's important to celebrate these habits as part of who they are.

3. Don't Take It Personally

There may be times when someone is late, disorganised, or needs to suddenly leave a social event. This isn't a reflection of you; it's a reflection of the way their brain functions. Changes in plans or overstimulating environments can frustrate people with ADHD.

It's not about you; they're simply trying to manage their sensory needs. To support these moments is how you best help them.

4. Recognise the Unique Strengths of Neurodivergence

People with ADHD and autism often bring incredible strengths to our community, including creativity, problem-solving. Their deep focus when they are passionate about something. Let's celebrate their strengths and ideas, even if they face difficulties.

As we work to foster a more inclusive and supportive environment, I encourage you all to approach neurodivergent individuals with understanding and patience. By being informed and compassionate, we can ensure that everyone in our community feels valued and respected for who they are.

You Are Not Alone: Stories of Dyslexia and Resilience

    Stories have the power to inspire and remind us we are not alone. In this book, I want to share the stories of dyslexics I have encountered throughout my journey within my family, my child, my community, and myself.

    The first step in sharing my story as a dyslexic adult was an emotional experience. You may recall that my journey of discovering I had dyslexia was inspired by my child, who struggled with speech development. Studying child development at university as a nurse, I learned that children who develop speech late may later be diagnosed with dyslexia. This was the case for my child.

    When I first heard the word "dyslexia," it was a lightbulb moment. It all made sense: my student difficulties with reading, spelling, and comprehension. I struggled with history's many dates and the extensive reading required for literature. The demands of reading and memorisation felt impossible. However, over time, by training my brain with the right tools, understanding how I learn as a visual learner. Self-awareness transformed me and helped me succeed.

I learned to store and recall information systematically in ways that worked for me. For example, if you tell me your name, I will try to match it with a place or scene to remember it. If you tell me a story, I will connect it to a past event or visualise it as a movie in my mind to help me retain the details. I also discovered how to tell my story and amplify the voices of others. To help others manage their challenges through my lived experiences

Recently, I have had several conversations about dyslexia and neurodiversity. In 2025, I started a podcast called *Dyslexia with Success*. One of my special guests was from America, and she shared a vivid testimony about living with both neurodiversity and dyslexia. It was a fascinating discussion as she spoke about both her successes and struggles as an adult with learning needs. She has multiple neurodivergent conditions and declared that she has ADHD as well as dyslexia. My guest also shared experiencing Narcolepsy.

In our conversation, she explained that her biggest supporter in her journey with dyslexia had been her mother. Her mother always encouraged her, appreciated her, and supported her, even when she faced challenges or when others laughed at her. For example, despite not having the greatest singing voice, her mother would tell her she was talented and enough. As an adult, she understands the immense impact of her mother's moral support and love. Perseverance and support helped her succeed; she's now an engineer working for workplace equality.

She talked about her ongoing struggles with reading and writing, which have never fully improved. Interestingly, she also speaks about her **time blindness**, a common challenge for people with dyslexia and ADHD. Despite waking up early, she still arrived late to work. One of the most powerful takeaways from our conversation was the strategy she put in place to help her function as an adult.

A friend who understood her struggles helped her break her daily routine into **15-minute time chunks**. When to wake up, shower, brush her teeth, eat, and get ready. This structured approach proved beneficial, allowing her to live a fully functional life as a neurodivergent adult. Structured routines can help people with dyslexia or ADHD succeed.

To stay on track, my friend. Who prefers to remain anonymous, uses her phone as an alarm system. Her alarms remind her when to take medication, attend appointments, and start her next activity.

Although structure is important for neurodivergent adults, too much can be negative, she testified. Working in an environment with rigid structures can be overwhelming. When neurodivergent individuals need a break but cannot step away, they may struggle, leading to burnout or failure.

One unique aspect of my thinking process is that I can juggle three conversations in my head simultaneously. For example, I could be on the phone discussing one topic while typing something unrelated and constructing a mental story about what I need to do before the day ends. Talking, typing, and planning, none of them connected, yet I can juggle them all. It can get even more complex, but I know I am not alone in this mind-mapping way of functioning. This ability enhances my productivity, but sometimes, if there is a disruption, I might accidentally say something unrelated to the person on the phone.

This is the power of understanding your unique gifts and learning how to use them to your advantage. The pandemic also played a role in my self-discovery, as I took time for deep reflection and wrote several quotes, which I will share in the appendix of this book.

Growing up in Cameroon, dyslexia was never discussed. Determined to change this, I founded the **Cameroon Dyslexia Association** to raise awareness. Throughout my journey, I engaged with key stakeholders. The governor, social services, education delegates, the Ministry of Social Affairs, and national media were included. As an opportunity to sensitise my community. However, time and time again, I was asked the same frustrating question: *Can you prove that dyslexia exists?*

One moment that stood out was meeting the Ministry of Social Affairs in Douala. When I arrived for my appointment, the receptionist saw my badge and said, "I'm dyslexic." I was surprised she was the first Cameroonian I had ever met who openly identified as dyslexic. Most people I spoke to either denied their dyslexia or feared being labelled as unintelligent. She shared her childhood difficulties with spatial awareness and understanding directions. Even as an adult, she still found it challenging. After years of searching online, she finally discovered that her struggles had a name: dyslexia. She was amazed that I was there to speak to her boss about it. Before heading into my meeting, I thanked her for sharing her story and invited her to speak at a future event.

The Reality of Dyslexia: A Story from the UK

Another powerful story comes from a woman I met in London. She is the founder of a dyslexia organisation in her West African home country. Over the years, we have connected through conferences and online meetings. She has allowed me to share her story in this book while keeping her identity anonymous.

When she moved to the UK with her mother and stepfather, English was her second language, making school even more challenging. She spent hours at the table struggling with homework, never able to finish. Her stepfather, frustrated by her difficulties, resorted to physical punishment. She was bullied and forced to do household chores instead of receiving support for her learning struggles.

One day, she confided in a teacher about her situation at home and her difficulty with schoolwork. This moment changed her life. Authorities intervened, and she was removed from her home and placed in children's services. However, her struggles with education continued, and she eventually dropped out of school.

Despite her challenges, she found a path forward. She had a natural talent for makeup artistry and pursued it as a trade. Job applications at large stores like Debenhams required English and math certificates, but she didn't have them. In desperation, she even considered using her brother's results to get hired. But when given the opportunity, she excelled. She could apply makeup expertly, even with her eyes closed.

Her story highlights a critical issue: employers often prioritise certificates over skills. Therefore, awareness about dyslexia is so important, not just for individuals, but for society as a whole. She heads a group that supports dyslexic children, giving them the help she wished she'd had.

The Importance of Dyslexia Awareness

The person writing the foreword for this book also has dyslexia, and she was touched by the stories I have shared. My publisher, too, has a close loved one who is dyslexic. Considering that

20% of the world's population has dyslexia, chances are that everyone knows someone with dyslexia, whether they realise it or not.

One key concept I discuss in this book is **body doubling,** a simple yet effective strategy for dyslexics or neurodivergent individuals. Body doubling is having your mum or dad supporting when you are going to do sport or presentation, or a friend who sits with you and you do your work they don't need to tell what you need to write, your friend offers to type for you to help you complete your dissertation on time because you are behind with university work, You husband sit with you when you are cooking or doing the laundry, these family friends, or teacher telling you well done, you can do, you are good enough, you have done your best, don't worry too much. Struggling is acceptable and a normal part of life. Affirmations are crucial support that neurodivergent individuals require, as essential as water and food. Having a light conversation gives you the motivation and is good moral support. Sometimes, we don't need someone to teach us what to do, just to be present as another; we just need someone present to keep us on track. A supportive and understanding community, not a judgmental one, is best for people with dyslexia.

About The Author

Petronila Asang Ngeka was born in Bamenda, Cameroon. She is an entrepreneur, Award-winning author, Podcaster, founder of Cameroon Dyslexia Association and CEO of Mcare24 Ltd care company. She gained a diploma in business management in 2008 and graduated from Anglia Ruskin University, Cambridge, in 2012 as an adult nurse. She has nursing experience in cardiothoracic critical care in Papworth Hospital, Cambridge and general ICU in Birmingham. Petronila has worked in the community as a CQC registered manager for her domiciliary care and a supported living care service provider for people with learning disabilities, and mental health and/or substance abuse issues. She featured on the BBC in 2019, the Voice Newspaper in 2022, CRTV in 2023 in Cameroon, Global Women magazine 2024 in London.

Petronila lives in Birmingham, UK, with her two children. She is very passionate about caring for people and believes in her efforts to make a change.

www.marciampublishinghouse.com

www.ingramcontent.com/pod-product-compliance
Lightning Source LLC
Chambersburg PA
CBHW011420070526
44584CB00026BA/3780